TALKING WITH KIDS

How to improve communication — and your relationship — with your children

ALISON MULVANEY

MEDIA MASTERS
SINGAPORE

TALKING WITH KIDS

© 1995 Text: Alison Mulvaney
© 1995 Illustrations: Mark David

Published by Media Masters Pte Ltd
Newton Road PO Box 272
Singapore 912210
Fax (65) 484 2559
E-mail: medmas@mbox3.singnet.com.sg

Published in October, 1998, by agreement
with Simon & Schuster Australia

Book design by Joy Ackerman
Cover design by Media Masters Pte Ltd
Printed in Singapore by Mui Kee Press & Co.

Distributed exclusively throughout the United Kingdom
 by John Wilson Booksales, 1 High Street,
Princes Risborough, Bucks HP27 OAG.
Telephone (44) (01844) 275 927; Fax (44) (01844) 274402

[The pronouns 'she' and 'he' have been used alternately in the chapters of this
book.] For information about Talking With Kids Workshops, please contact
Alison Mulvaney on (61) (02) 98992094.

ISBN 981-04-0734-3

Contents

Introduction

This book has come out of my passion for children. Over the past 10 years of working with children I have learned so much from them and have realised what an incredible contribution they make to our lives. They add original thought, they add joy, and most of all, they add sparkle. There may be some readers who are at this very moment remembering the time that young Tommy spread peanut butter all over the wallpaper and the new lounge suite and who are thinking that I am totally mad. Nevertheless, despite the ups and downs of living with and caring for children, most people would agree that, overall, children add more to our lives than less. More love, more laughter, and a multitude of opportunities for learning new things about ourselves and how we interact with others. In fact, I always liken my experience with children to one big birthday party. It's full of surprises.

Not only do children have a marked effect upon us as adults, we have a very significant effect upon them while they are in our care and beyond into adulthood. We are continually involving ourselves in the process of educating our children. Our every word, thought and action, no matter how large or small, expresses something to the children around us. We are their role models and as role models we have a weighty responsibility. Unfortunately, a child is not born with an instruction manual carried under one arm, and when something goes wrong, it's often the parent who gets the blame. Parents on the whole are blamed and *not* trained. There is no other job I know of where, usually, two individuals are handed a strange package they have never seen before and where they have to make this package into a happy, successful one, but are given no instructions about how to do it. Ready, set, go!

Over the years, I have been fortunate enough to observe the family dynamics and communication patterns of thousands of children and their families. By their nature, communication handicaps usually require long-term intervention and so I have been in this unique position of observer over very lengthy periods of time for each child and her family, sometimes up to four or five years or more. Of course, from the vantage point of independent observer, it is always easier to see where any breakdown occurs.

In all families, breakdown in communication occurs at one time or another. Using my skills as a communication specialist and a psychotherapist, I have been able to gain some insights into the nature of these breakdowns and develop some remedies that I believe are useful in both avoiding breakdowns and repairing them.

So this book is about filling in the gaps in knowledge that you need to avoid the pitfalls, to be able to patch them up if and when they do occur and, hopefully, to make both the life of your child and your life as the adult caretaker easier, more enjoyable and more successful.

In this book you will have the opportunity to explore your own values, beliefs, feelings and attitudes towards yourself and others and, most of all, to closely examine and improve your own communication patterns. You will discover where these patterns have come from and how miscommunication can so easily occur between yourself and your child. Classic communication patterns between individuals are explored, as are the barriers that might prevent us from learning, changing and developing new skills.

An important chapter in the book is Chapter 6, which deals with suggestions for handling both your own and your child's emotions. Detailed practical examples are given on how to make the changes that you need to make in order to have great communication and a very healthy and happy relationship. Chapter 9 shows you how to help your child set goals and how to teach her values, an essential gift for any child of today. This book is in part experiential and I would encourage you to fully participate in it and jump right in.

But first!

I wonder, as an author, what gaps *you* may need to have filled in in your caretaking of that special package called a child. We all have different reasons for reading books. Some of us want to be entertained, some of us want to learn new information and some of us already have information and we simply want to check its accuracy. If you were to think carefully about your reasons for reading this particular book I wonder what you might come up with.

Sometimes it makes it easier for us to identify our own situations by reading about the situations of others, and so to help you in thinking about your reasons for reading this book I have included some simple case histories of other people's situations. These parents and teachers may be in a similar situation to you.

You may feel like Martha.

Martha was 23 years of age and a single parent. She was living in a situation where she had no family support and she came to a Talking with Kids seminar (designed for parents and teachers to enhance communication skills with children, thus helping to boost the child's motivation and self-esteem) because her three-year-old was taxing every last bit of her strength. Martha was aware that she was spending most of her time literally screaming at him. She was looking for a way out of the screaming cycle that had been created. She wanted less stress and a better relationship with her son.

Maybe you think like John.

John was a computer programmer with two teenage children. He had a good relationship with both of them and yet he never felt that he could talk to them on their wavelength. To John, it was as though his children spoke a different language that he couldn't translate. John wanted to improve the quality of his contact and the quality of his communication with his children and so he came to me for professional advice.

Perhaps you identify with Shirley?

Shirley had a teaching diploma and she was working on her master's degree in education. She couldn't understand why she was having so much difficulty in getting through to her children and was becoming really frustrated about not being heard. She thought that someone with her background and training should be able to get her own children to do what she wanted them to do. Shirley had all of the theory and what she needed were down-to-earth practical tips on how to change the communication patterns that she was currently using to ones that would bring her better results.

Do you sound like David?

David was a busy corporate executive who spent a great deal of time away from his family. He came to me with the problem of how to find a way to motivate his eldest son to study for his exams. David had even promised his son a new personal computer as a reward, but in David's eyes his son just didn't seem to have the get up and go that he wanted him to have. David wanted to find some way of getting his son to work for his own goals.

Can you relate to Lisa?

Lisa was a housewife with two primary school-aged children. She knew that she had good communication skills. What she didn't understand was why her children constantly ignored her requests to clean up their rooms or to turn down the television. She was telling them in a way that let them know they had better move *or else* and was truly astonished that it never seemed to work. Lisa came to me as a friend and it was very clear that she wanted to know what she was doing wrong and how she could get her children to listen to her.

Perhaps you can see yourself in the same shoes as Lisa, or maybe David sounds like someone you can relate to. Perhaps you feel the same as Shirley. Whichever scenario holds true for you, it's useful to identify the unique qualities of your own scenarios and the questions and answers that apply to your own personal situation.

If you were to think about your own scenarios where you are having difficulty in communicating with your children or where you feel that you are communicating really well, what would they be? If you had questions that you wanted this book to answer what would those questions be? In short, what do you want to get out of reading this book?

Often when we become clear on what we want, it makes it so much easier to find the solutions to our problems.

I would not suggest for one moment that this book has all the answers that you need, since no book ever will. I do know that it will certainly help you in discovering a large part of the answers you need and how to implement them. I do know that the techniques described in this book have helped Martha change her relationship with her three-year-old; they have helped John really relate and talk to his children on the same wavelength; they have helped Shirley gain practical skills that work both at home and at school; they have helped David motivate his 10-year-old son to do schoolwork; and they have helped Lisa to get her children to not only listen to her, but to talk with her about themselves and their lives. So whether you are a parent, teacher, grandparent or a caretaker of children in any way, my wish is that this book will provide you with the insights and the skills that you need to make your interactions with children much easier, more successful, more joyful and more fun.

Not only will you learn a whole lot more about communicating with children, you will learn about communicating more successfully with yourself and other adults as well.

Happy reading.

CHAPTER ONE

What Is Communication?

When we think of communication we often think of it as nothing more than giving or receiving a message. Of course this is absolutely true, but when we look at communication more closely we realise that it is in fact much more important than this. I would have no hesitation in saying that communication is the most important aspect of our daily lives. You may be thinking, well, she's biased because that's her job and specialty area, so of course she's going to think communication is the most important thing in the world. If you really think about it though, we could not survive without some form of communication.

We communicate to form our relationships with our parents, grandparents, children, friends, bosses and co-workers. We communicate to maintain these relationships with others. How would we become educated or educate others if it weren't for communication? Would we find it so easy to get food, clothing and shelter if we couldn't communicate? How would we do business with others and how would we relax and have recreation times if we couldn't communicate our needs? To me, communicating is just as important as breathing, and therefore I would not be doing justice to this book and to you, the reader, if I didn't look more closely with you into what communication really is. So let's see what communicating is really about.

The act of communication involves the expression of yourself. It says to the world 'This is who I am'. It is our way of expressing our beliefs, our values and our feelings.

Not only does the content of what we communicate matter, the way in which we communicate these beliefs, values and feelings is essential to our lives. That is, it's not just what we say, it's how we say it. Communication can be broken down into verbal communication and non-verbal communication. The verbal communication is the words that we use in our message and the non-verbal communication is the body language and the underlying meaning that we have in our message. Many of us focus only on the words that we need to use and forget that the underlying message, facial expression, tone of voice and hand gestures are vitally important in getting our message across clearly and successfully. In fact, researcher into human behaviour Albert Mehrabian found that the total impact of a message is about 7 per cent verbal and 55 per cent non-verbal and that the verbal component of a face-to-face conversation is less than 35 per cent. Over 65 per cent of a face-to-face conversation is done through non-verbal communication.

We will be learning more about how we communicate non-verbally later on, but first let us look at *what* we are communicating and *why* we are communicating it.

When we talk about communicating with our children we need to be clear in our minds as to *why* we are communicating with them. What's the purpose? Why do we bother doing it? My personal list of reasons for communicating with children can be summed up pretty simply in one phrase: 'Communication is to relationship what breathing is to living.' In other words, I communicate with children to form a relationship with them. If I were to get even more specific about that relationship I would say that I communicate with children to educate, nurture, negotiate, motivate, reward and love them. Quite a list, isn't it!

Why Are You Communicating?

If you were to consider the reasons why you communicate with your children or the children that you care for, what would they be?

Go ahead and list your reasons on a sheet of paper.

Before now, could it be that many of us have never really thought about our reasons for communicating and therefore parenting our children? If you have no goal then it's difficult to develop a communication style that will encourage your children to develop as human beings. The *goal* is the *outcome* that we are trying to achieve, and the way in which we communicate is the *how* of how we achieve our outcome. That is to say, my goal may be to empower my child to maturity and I do this by nurturing, educating, negotiating with, rewarding and loving my child.

Many professionals believe that the following goal is the most useful goal to have in parenting children. Let's see if you agree.

Our goal as parents is to empower our children to become mature and to release them to become independent.

While agreeing with this statement, many parents actually find it difficult to fulfil the last part of the statement — releasing their children. When a parent holds on too tightly to a child, it's usually because he's trying to meet his own needs instead of the child's needs. Parents who are controlling and disabling always jump in with helping comments such as 'Here, that's too hard for you, let me do it'. Many parents even speak for the child, constantly answering for him. These types of responses actually handicap the child because they make him feel that he's incapable of doing things for himself. True parental empowerment allows the child to feel adequate and it empowers him to maturity.

One of the most dramatic images of a parent encouraging a child

to spread his wings and fly is the eagle. When the mother eagle draws courage from her wisdom and realises that until her children discover their wings there is no true purpose for their lives, she pushes them off the cliff face. The young eagle spreads its wings and catches an updraught. It learns how to flap its wings and how to hunt for food and eventually it leaves the nest to make its own home.

Like the baby eagle there comes a time when our children need to be physically and emotionally set free from our control. If we don't do this we can cause ourselves to be handicapped as parents. If we make our children so necessary to our own happiness then we grow incapable of managing without them.

You may find as parents that if you don't release your children to independence and thus fulfil the second part of the goal, negative consequences may occur. The child may continue to be unnaturally dependent on you or may totally rebel against your control, breaking away from the family, perhaps permanently. Therefore it's useful to have a clear set of goals for parenting and a clear set of reasons as to why we are communicating with our children.

What Are We Communicating?

Now let's look at *what* we are communicating. We communicate our knowledge, beliefs, values and feelings to our children.

Our beliefs are the things we believe to be true. They are the way that we interpret the world around us. For example, I have a belief that the sun will come up every morning and set every evening. Many people believe there is a God, while many others believe that mothers always love their children. From this we can see that we as individuals probably have a lot of beliefs about ourselves, our children, our relatives, friends, neighbours and in fact everyone and everything in our world.

Believe it or not, we hold a lot of beliefs about ourselves as communicators, too. Every day we see, hear, and feel evidence that supports these beliefs about ourselves.

If you were to take the time to actually sit down and list some of the beliefs that you hold about yourself as a communicator, I wonder what you might discover. Do you consider yourself to be a good communicator or a bad communicator? If you are good at communicating, exactly what is it that you do that makes you a good communicator? In what contexts or situations do you communicate easily? Why is that? Do you know? If you consider yourself to be a poor communicator, what do you think you are doing that is making your communications unsuccessful? Are there particular contexts or situations in which you communicate better than in others? Before you take the time to list the beliefs you have about yourself as a communicator, you might find it useful to read the list of beliefs set out below as well as what others have listed about their relationship to communication.

Here are some of the beliefs that people have about themselves in relation to communication:

- Every time I open my mouth I put my foot in it.
- I'm just no good with words.
- I can talk my way out of anything.

- I really have the gift of the gab.
- If I keep my opinions to myself then I can never be wrong.
- I'm not giving anything away.
- I don't understand.
- I've got to be right no matter whom I'm talking to.
- I can never ask for what I want.
- Notice me — I'm the loud one.
- What's the point in speaking up?
- I never get heard.
- Nobody ever listens to what I have to say.
- I'm always getting ready to say something (but I'm not ready yet).
- I don't need to tell you what I'm thinking, you should just know.

Remember Martha, the 23-year-old single parent? Martha sat down and wrote out the beliefs she held about herself as a communicator. They were as follows:

> I can't believe I'm writing this, but I scream most of the time rather than talk, especially with my three-year-old.
>
> I don't think I'm a good communicator when it comes to my children and my own parents because I don't really listen to them properly.
>
> I'm a good communicator with my girlfriends. I understand what they're talking about, where they're coming from. I feel like I'm on the same wavelength as them.
>
> I don't communicate very much at all at work. I'm too scared to speak up and say what I think because I think they'll just laugh at me and tell me that I'm wrong.

This is what John the computer programmer had to say:

> I'm really clear about what I say at work. I always listen to people and nine times out of ten they get my message clearly. I guess I feel confident communicating with my workmates and superiors. I'm

never afraid to communicate new ideas that I have because I know my bosses are good communicators and they will always listen to what I have to say. I'm not as confident communicating at home. I always think that my kids find what I have to say really boring. I never really get their attention. I suppose when they've come to talk to me, I've always been too busy to listen. Maybe they're scared to talk to me.

Shirley the teacher had this to say:

I always let the kids at school know who is boss from the very first day. All I have to do is shout at them and they listen. I believe that works fine most of the time.

I do notice that it's never clear whether they understand me or not because they don't seem that eager to put up their hands and ask questions. Maybe I threaten them too much, but I believe children should be seen and not heard. My own kids at home never do what I ask them to do, no matter how much I groan and complain. Maybe I need to do more about the way I talk to them, but I just don't know what I need to change or how to do it. I've been doing it this way for so long.

David the corporate executive had a very different story:

I do professional presentations to clients all the time and I think I'm a good communicator. I look them in the eye, I speak clearly and I make them feel relaxed when I talk to them. I even manage to throw in some humour from time to time so they know that business doesn't have to be too serious.

I'm pretty good at communicating with my wife and kids. I know that because they always come and ask my advice about things. I try and make regular time each week to sit down and talk about things with my wife and I plan to start doing that with the kids too because it's working out really well. Yes. I'm a good communicator 90 per cent of the time.

So now, having read these examples, go ahead and write down some of your own beliefs about yourself as a communicator. They can be simple sentences or small scenarios similar to our case studies.

Beliefs about Children

It's also valuable to identify beliefs that we have about ourselves as parents, as well as beliefs that we hold about our own children or children in general.

Let's look at children first. Do you believe, like Shirley, that children should be seen and not heard? Do you believe that children should be treated as equals? Do you believe that children should be given strict guidelines on behaviour and that they should be given strict values to live by?

Before you write down your beliefs about your own children or children in general, browse through the beliefs listed below.

- Children are a joy.
- Children should be seen and not heard.
- Boys will be boys.
- Little girls should be little ladies.
- Children should do as they are told.
- Children should respect their elders.
- My child never interferes with my life.
- Life is a struggle when you have kids.
- Children are at their best when they're asleep.
- Children should be loved and respected for who they are.
- I treat my children as individuals.
- Never talk down to children.
- Always give in to children.
- Children are helpless.
- Children will always push you to your limit.
- Never let your children get the upper hand.

- Always keep your children under control.
- My children have perfect manners.
- My children are smarter than yours.
- Once you've got kids, you're stuck with them for life.

Now list your own beliefs about children.

Beliefs about Parenting

Now having done that, I'd like you to consider the following question: What beliefs do you hold about yourself as a parent, teacher, grandparent or caregiver? Do you believe that you are an effective parent, teacher and so on, and if so, why are you effective? If you're not 100 per cent effective as a caregiver of children, then in what areas are you not so effective? Do you know why?

What beliefs do you hold about yourself as a parent? (If you're not a parent then simply substitute the title that applies to you.)

Here are some common beliefs held by parents:

- Parenting is a huge responsibility.
- Parenting isn't meant to be fun.
- Parents are always worn to a frazzle.
- Dads should be the ones to discipline the children.
- Children should be smacked.
- Children should never be smacked.
- It's the mother's responsibility to look after the children.
- It's the father's responsibility to provide for the family.
- Being a parent is fun.
- Being a parent is an honour.
- Being a parent is a joy.
- Children are not our possessions.
- Children are our greatest teachers.
- You should always be nice to children.
- Children should be protected from the real world.
- Nobody loves a whingeing child.

- Nobody loves a naughty child.
- I don't understand children.
- I'd be a hopeless mother/father.
- Children should always be good and helpful.
- If I ignore my children they leave me alone.
- You can't ever win with kids.

Now go ahead and list your beliefs about being a caregiver of children along with the reasons why you are effective or ineffective as a caregiver.

The Beliefs of Others

If you are in a partnership the beliefs of the other person will directly affect how you parent as a twosome.

If you have a partner, what beliefs do you think that your partner holds about being a parent? Of course, in this instance, unless you actually ask your partner, you are assuming that these are his or her beliefs. Write your assumptions about your partner's beliefs and then compare them with your own beliefs about parenting. Do these two lots of beliefs match up in any way or not? Can you see any conflicts of beliefs and how do they manifest themselves in your effectiveness as parents? When we get to this point in the Talking with Kids workshop, the parents are always eager to sort out their differences and find a way to come to some alignment on their beliefs. Sometimes this isn't possible and they just have to accept that their partner has differing beliefs from them. It's the differences that make us interesting as human beings after all. In Chapter 3 'Miscommunication: How Does it Happen?' we will be looking more closely at how to resolve these types of conflicts.

So you can see that exploring our beliefs is quite a revealing process. The results of this exploration tell us a great deal about ourselves and the skills with which we communicate, teach or parent. If you were to form a summary of the most important things that you learned about yourself from doing this exercise what would they be? Write down your summary.

Your Life Values

In communicating we also express our values. These are the things that are most important to us, the things that motivate us and the things that help us decide whether our actions are good or bad. For example, I may place a high value on creativity because I am a writer. Other people may place a high value on fun, or money, or good health, or travel or love. We all have values and they play a very important role in how we communicate who we are to the outside world.

If you were to list the 10 most important qualities in your life that you value what would they be? But first let's look at the values lists of some of our case study parents.

Martha listed the following 10 most important values in her life: friends, fun, relaxation, honesty, money, love, family, holidays, music, art.

John had quite a different list: marriage, business, honesty, travel, wealth, success, friendship, sport, health, enjoyment.

Shirley's list was different again: holidays, money, literature, knowledge, trust, family, friendship, entertainment, love, work.

Go ahead and list your 10 most important values in life.

Values in Your Relationship with Your Children

If you look closely at these values you will see that they are reflected in certain areas of your life. If friends and relaxation are high on your list then maybe you do a lot of entertaining. If money is high on your list then maybe your main focus is on the business part of your life. If knowledge and literature are important to you, my guess would be that you have quite a library of books at home.

Now consider the five values that you hold to be the most important in relationship to your children or the children that you work with. Before you do that, let's read some of the lists of our case study parents.

Martha listed the following five qualities as her most important values with children: love, joy, friendship, education, discipline.

John's list was as follows: love, sharing, teaching, guiding, fun.

Shirley's list contained the following values: disciplining, teaching, providing, achieving, caring.

David's list was as follows: success, motivating, providing, sharing, love.

Now go ahead and list your five most important values in relationship to your children or the children that you care for. Notice what you learn about yourself from looking at your list of values. Do the values reflect how you have parented your children? Do your values reflect how you communicate with your children?

My guess is that they would do just that. Values play a very important role in our lives.

My own personal values in relation to children are: loving, sharing, empowering, rewarding and educating.

If I were to find one single value that encompasses all of these qualities I would choose the value of 'educating'. When we love, share, empower, and reward our children we are always in some form or another involving ourselves in the process of 'educare'; that is, educating. Every word we say and every thing that we do and every emotion that we express educates our children about living in this world today. Whether we are a teacher, a parent, a grandparent or any role model for a child, we are educating them with our words, our actions and, sometimes, our very thoughts. Of course, there is so much information available to us on how to relate to children that we can easily be overwhelmed by the advice of all the experts. When it comes down to it, the quality of our relationship with our children is totally dependent upon our ability to communicate with them. When we communicate with them we are communicating our own beliefs about ourselves and them, and our own values about life and children in general.

It is true to say then that we bring to any communication with our children a great deal of ourselves and our personal history. When we are made aware of our beliefs and values we can sometimes glean the reasons for the success or failure of our communications and our relationships with our children. When we learn to communicate and truly make contact with our children, the rest is easy. Then and only then is it easy to motivate them, nurture them, negotiate with them, avoid misunderstandings and frustrations, and just love them.

With the pressures upon both children and parents today, this is not always easy.

Let's explore this further.

Pressures upon Parents

Mat and Bev have been married for 10 years. They and their two children, Tom, aged eight, and Sarah, aged six, live in a new housing development on the outskirts of the western Sydney suburbs. Mat has to travel at least two hours every day to get to work and back again and Bev has recently gone back to work as a preschool teacher.

Mat has been worried about work. He has been with the same company for 15 years, but over the past 18 months business has really dropped off. Many of his workmates have been retrenched and Mat is worried that he might be the next to go. Bev's job is only temporary as she is covering for another teacher on maternity leave. Understandably, they were both a little worn out and worried. One night Bev had rushed home from work to get the dinner ready, but it wasn't ready when Mat got home and he was tired and hungry and not impressed. Sarah wanted to show Dad what she had made at school that day, but Mat wasn't interested as he had a lot on his mind. Bev was annoyed and nagged him about never having any time for the children. An argument followed and by the time everyone sat down to dinner you could cut the air with a knife.

I don't know if there was ever a time when parenting was truly simple. I don't believe so. I do believe, however, that parents today are faced with even more pressure than in previous years. These pressures appear to come from three main areas — themselves, their work and their relationship with their partner. Of course, single parenting brings with it the pressure of not having any partner to help you with your parenting responsibilities.

Parents can and often do experience financial burdens, the threat of possible retrenchment and unemployment and the pressures that come from the responsibilities that working brings. You have a boss to answer to or at least someone superior to you, or you are self-employed and incur all of the worries of being your own boss. Like Bev, women often have two jobs to deal with: both the running of the home and the care of children and a husband, and also their other job that in itself may have all of the demands outlined above. All parents want their children to have the best and that includes ballet lessons, cricket clubs, videos, parties, holidays. And the list goes on and on. All of these things cost money. The pressures of earning enough to support a lifestyle can result in symptoms of impatience and withdrawal. Single parents have the difficulty of finding and maintaining out-of-school care for their children. This in itself can be costly. Not to mention the difficulty of taking time off work if a child becomes ill or has an accident. Not all employers take kindly to employees taking time off work to look after sick children. This can make the parent feel insecure about their ability to keep their job. Work and family are often in direct competition with one another.

By the time you get home from work you can often feel drained of energy. You certainly have to draw on your reserves in your fuel tank to get the house chores done and find time to take the children to their appointments, help with homework and still find time to play with and discipline them. It's exhausting just thinking about it.

Not only are there the responsibilities to your professional life and to your family but the responsibility to yourself. Finding time for yourself can seem like such a challenge when you're a busy person. Not only do you need to find time for yourself but also time for your spouse so that your relationship continues to develop. It's difficult to care for and love your children if you don't feel loved and cared for by your partner. Any relationship in itself requires work.

In addition to these three areas of pressure there is also the responsibility that we have to our own parents if they are still with us and also the challenge of finding the time for our friends. Most people would agree that life in the 1990s brings with it many stresses and new challenges of how to achieve a balance in life.

And parents aren't the only ones to suffer from the pressures that today's society faces us with. Let's look now at the pressures that children encounter in their lives.

Pressures upon Children

Julie was a very popular eight-year-old who always did well at school and related pretty well with her two brothers, Adam and James. Julie had high expectations for herself both in the academic areas of school and in school sports. Every year she made the A-grade netball team and every year she came in the top three of the class. This year she seemed to be so stressed out by her overladen schedule that by the time she came to the end-of-year exams she was suffering from phantom stomach cramps that turned out to be an ulcer. This kept her off school for days at a time so that she missed important school work and her grades dropped dramatically because she was always so tired from her weekly commitments. By the end of the week she would argue constantly and noisily with both her brothers. Julie was certainly not experiencing a balanced lifestyle.

As you can see from Julie's story, children have just as many pressures upon them as we do. Their pressures are just a little different from ours. They have pressures from school, family, themselves and their peers. Pressures from school can include the pressure of pleasing the teacher, performing to expectations of both the teacher and their parents and also establishing friendships and keeping them. At a time when they are most sensitive to being hurt, it seems that children are not always as sensitive to the hurt that they cause. Children can be pretty destructive when it comes to other children's self-esteem. The pressure from peers can be enormous at any age and the desire to be accepted is very strong in young children. Some children, like young Julie, place very high standards upon themselves even at a very young age. These can include academic standards, sporting standards, high standards in other recreational activities and even friendship standards. Children who place unrealistic expectations upon themselves often share a number of self-limiting beliefs, some of which are as follows:

- I have to be the best.
- Mum and Dad won't love me unless I come first.
- I'll die if I don't make the team.
- I have to be like everyone else, otherwise they won't like me.
- I'm only worthwhile if I win.
- I need to impress my friends.

We as adults who care for children must acknowledge that we bring to our communications with our children not only our beliefs and values, but also the feelings that we have associated with our own personal pressures. The children that we care for bring in turn their personal beliefs, values and pressures to any communication with us. All of this needs to be taken into account when we are looking at achieving successful communications. One thing that seems to be of utmost importance in all of this is *congruency*. This means that what we think, feel, say and do all match up together. Let's look more closely at the area of feelings.

Feelings

Are you aware that even without saying a word it's very easy to communicate a feeling to a child. Children are by their nature far more intuitive than we. Haven't you noticed that your child seems to know exactly the sort of behaviour that's going to drive you nuts, get your back up and most definitely get a reaction from you! It's almost like they have a built-in radar that says, 'Yes, this is what I need to do to get a response'.

Unfortunately for some children any response is better than no response, so desperate are they for some attention. Have you ever noticed how your children just seem to know when you're feeling down. Sometimes they come and put their arms around you and say, 'Don't be sad' when you haven't even mentioned a thing and in fact you thought you were putting on a brave front for their benefit. Children are highly intuitive when it comes to feelings. Give them the merest hint of an underlying emotion and, like a sniffer dog, they can sniff it out. What, you may wonder, does this have to do with communication? The answer to that is, 'Everything'. If we don't even have to open our mouths to communicate our feelings to our children, how good must they be at picking a fake statement a mile off? This is where congruency comes in.

Have you ever told a child a story that wasn't true and winced under the scrutiny of their big accusing eyes? Children have an in-built 'bull barometer', which is why we have to be congruent when we communicate with them. We will be talking about congruency in greater detail in later chapters.

We communicate a range of feelings to our children including anger, sadness, fear, love and acceptance. When you communicate with your child, regardless of what you say, your child knows how you *really* feel. Therefore there is absolutely no point in trying to hide your feelings from your child, or trying to communicate something different on the surface. This would be *incongruency*. Parents are not perfect and they never will be, so why try to act like you approve or accept a child's behaviour if you don't? Why try to act happy if you're really depressed? Sure as anything that child will know, and once you're pinned as a faker it may be difficult for the child to trust you in other areas of your lives together. I'm sure you'll agree that the truth will be the best way to communicate with your child. Also, once the behaviour of incongruency, or covering up emotions, is firmly entrenched it can be quite a sticky situation to change. So it's best to establish honest relations as early as possible. I'm not advocating telling your child that there's no Santa Claus, I'm merely suggesting that you try to be as congruent as possible in your communications with your child.

Parents who are honest with their children are real parents; parents that their children will feel comfortable with talking about anything in the early days of their lives and in those difficult teenage years. If you already know that you've fallen into the habit of hiding your true feelings from your children, then go gently on yourself and gradually ease yourself into a change of behaviour. It doesn't mean that you've been a bad parent.

After all, you were probably doing it because you thought that you were protecting your children. So make the commitment to at least start to change the behaviours that you currently use so that you can move towards becoming more congruent. Perhaps you could pick a situation to practise in, for instance, at the dinner table. Every night at the dinner table try making a concerted effort to be honest with your children even if it means that they get sulky or cranky with you. Once you can communicate comfortably in this situation then extend it to others. Eventually, you'll find yourself unconsciously using a whole new behaviour where your feelings, thoughts, actions and words all match up to present a picture that is honest. Take your time and go slow if you need to. You can't change old habits overnight.

Remember, parents aren't trained for their job — they learn on the job. Here's your chance to use some information that will add value to your relationship with your child. Work towards becoming congruent. Why not give it a go!

My hope is that by reading this chapter and completing the exercises contained therein, that you will have gained some insights into your own beliefs, values and expression of feelings and how they relate to your communication patterns.

Store this information away for use in later chapters. Meanwhile, let's move on to Chapter 2 where we will be looking at answering the highly controversial question, 'When does communication begin?'.

But first, here is a handy summary of Chapter 1 for your use.

Key Points

❖ Communication is much more than just giving and receiving a message.

❖ Communication is made up of both verbal and non-verbal components.

❖ It's most useful to have a goal for communicating with your children; for example, communicating clearly and with a positive focus; or communicating to build self-esteem.

❖ Many experts believe that we as parents need to empower our children to maturity and then release them to independence.

❖ We communicate our knowledge, beliefs, values and feelings to our children.

❖ It's most useful to be congruent and honest in our communications with our children.

❖ It's important to remember that both parents and children are under pressure and that they bring feelings resulting from these pressures to their communications with one another.

CHAPTER TWO

When Does Communication Begin? How Did We Learn to Communicate?

Most of us have spent our lives believing that babies don't really communicate with us until they start to speak in recognisable words when they are about one year old. As a speech pathologist, I can tell you that this is a long way from the truth.

Babies begin to communicate verbally as early as three to four months of age. They are communicating with us through the sounds that they make and this continues on up until approximately nine months, when they extend this communication to long strings of connected sounds. What is truly amazing is that during this stage in a child's communication development she can produce every single sound of every language in existence. Isn't that extraordinary? The baby then moves on to producing single words and then small sentences that grow in complexity until the child reaches five years of age, at which time 90 per cent of the language has already been developed.

However, much much more occurs in the child long before she produces a single word. As a speech pathologist, it has always fascinated me that the child developed so many communication skills that involved the understanding of language long before she ever produced a word. From this fascination came a deep interest in the earliest forms of communication that exist between children and their mothers, even while the baby is unborn.

You may have seen the occasional documentary where pregnant mothers are talking to their unborn babies and even in some cases teaching them to read before they're born. In the late 1960s and 1970s, a new generation of medical technology meant that investigators in the area of what is called 'pre-natal psychology' were able to study the child undisturbed in the womb. This research revealed a dramatically different picture of the communication that occurs between the mother and the baby in the womb than that previously understood. Up until this time, the unborn baby was portrayed as a mindless, passive creature that could no sooner communicate with us than fly.

The written work of Dr Thomas Verny in *The Secret Life of the Unborn Child* is one of the few works available in this country on this particular area. Dr Verny admits that most of the research that went on in the 1960s and 1970s was pure clinical research and that the scientists weren't particularly interested in the practical applications of their findings. These findings do, however, have enormous implications for parenting, and for that reason I couldn't write this book without at least addressing this area in some small way. This research has too many implications for the lives of the children of today to be ignored. It is also regarded as highly controversial information.

Dr Verny's book is the product of six years of intensive study, thought, research and travel. He travelled worldwide to talk with the leading psychiatrists, psychologists, physiologists, obstetricians, foetologists and paediatricians throughout the world. The conclusions based upon research of these health professionals were as follows:

The foetus can see, hear, experience, taste, and learn on a primitive level, in the uterus before birth. Most importantly he can feel. His feelings are not on the advanced level that an adult feels but nevertheless he does feel.

These feelings and the things that the child perceives through sight, sound and taste begin shaping his attitudes and expectations about himself. The chief source of these shaping messages comes from the mother. (Page 34)

The mother's experience of emotions such as joy, anticipation and love may contribute significantly to the emotional development of the baby. Researchers such as Dr Verny further believe that continual feelings of ambivalence, mistrust and fear about the birth of the baby could cause personality problems later on in the child.

The father's feelings about his wife and his unborn child are highly significant in determining the success of the pregnancy and play a large part in the mother's emotions, which in turn affect the baby.

In July 1994 the *Sydney Morning Herald* reported a study conducted at Sydney Royal Hospital for Women that confirms Dr Verny's findings and many pregnant women's reports. The study involved 60 pregnant women between 36 and 40 weeks pregnant. These women were shown a video of the movie *Sophie's Choice*, in which the actress Meryl Streep plays a highly distraught mother. They were closely monitored for an hour before the film, during it and for an hour afterwards. After 20 minutes of watching the video, the foetuses started kicking and their heartbeat was raised. This only occurred if the movie upset the foetus's mother. This unpublished study showed once again that maternal conditions influence foetal behaviour.

In summary, Dr Verny and other leading health professionals in the area of pre-natal psychology believe that the way in which the baby is influenced in the uterus may shape the rest of the baby's life. That is pretty staggering information, isn't it?

This information deepens the importance of the role of a parent, and unlike genetic inheritance, factors such as the emotional stability and security of the mother, and the amount of support from the father during pregnancy as well as his feelings about the mother and unborn child can be controlled by the mother and the father. This doesn't mean that a child's future depends upon the mother thinking bright and positive thoughts 24 hours a day, but it does mean that she is able to favourably influence her baby in a way which the medical world previously thought impossible. This new knowledge also enhances the part that the father plays during pregnancy. It makes the father feel important and far more connected with the child earlier on, and this can only be a positive for their developing relationship. In turn the baby is positively affected by the father's expression of love and warmth. It can form the basis of a psychologically stable relationship between the two, not to mention the benefit in establishing a fully integrated psychological state in the child.

So how does this shaping of personality occur? The answer is through communication. Based on this research, it seems that this early form of non-verbal communication *in utero* is one of the most important stages of communication we will ever experience in our lives as it has such a significant effect on our future personality.

The happiest kind of learning and communication that occurs before birth is that of verbal communication; that is, speech. Our speech patterns are highly individual and distinctive. Dr Henry Truby, Professor of Pediatrics, Linguistics and Anthropology at the University of Miami, discovered through his research that a baby copies its mother's speech patterns *in utero* thus learning to communicate as early as six months before birth. The study showed that babies will move their bodies to the rhythm of their mother's speech.

From a communication specialist's point of view, this is astounding research. It means that a mother can influence her child's development by talking to her while she is in the womb. The baby can hear and respond to what is being said — true communication. The soft, soothing talk of the mother also makes the baby feel loved

and wanted and even though she can't interpret the words, the baby responds to the emotional tone of the mother's voice.

Dr Verny believes, and I wholeheartedly agree, that if mothers were to start communicating with their babies before birth, it would represent a monumental beginning. This way, the baby wouldn't feel as though she were in a confined space, alone for five or six months without any emotional or intellectual stimulation.

So it is clear that there is value in beginning to communicate with a child *in utero* through both verbal and non-verbal means. It is also clear that Dr Verny believes that the child's personality is affected by the quality of this mother–child communication. This communication is an important part of the bonding process that occurs after birth. Bonding is the phenomenon that the medical profession acknowledges occurs when the mother and the child form a 'connection' at birth. It is said to be extremely beneficial to both the mother and the baby. Imagine the possibility of this bonding occurring prior to birth and the benefits of that. Not only can the mother bond with the child much earlier, but so can the father. Research indicates that a baby who is spoken to by the father *in utero* may respond to the father's voice even in the first hour or two of life and that the father's voice can be used to soothe the baby when distressed. That is, the baby responds emotionally to the father's voice. In the past, fathers were often given the image of being bumbling idiots when it came to babies, and thank goodness that image is changing. Now fathers are present at the delivery, and some fathers choose to look after their babies when the mother goes back to work.

This information also throws new light on the importance of the birthing procedure itself. The French obstetrician Dr Frederick Leboyer, argued that gentler birthing methods were necessary. The emotions of both the mother and the soon-to-be-born child are affected by the bright lights and cold impersonal atmosphere of a strictly traditional medical birth.

Due to these findings and others, more mothers of all ages are choosing gentler birthing methods for their child in order to ensure less birth trauma. This must have implications for the future psychological state of the child, given that she has feelings before birth. According to Dr Verny, although the baby is said to be unable to determine the shades of meaning that an adult can put into words and gestures, the baby is sensitive to remarkably subtle emotional nuances. Many researchers say that this ability exists from the moment of conception; however, the hard clinical evidence suggests that it is from six months *in utero* that the baby has these abilities. The baby can already remember, hear and even learn to kick to a given stimulus of a vibration.

Many health professionals agree that the communication that occurs within the womb can only effectively continue following the birth of the baby if she is in physical contact with the mother. Touch is almost the lifeline of the communication process between the mother and the baby. Thank goodness birthing procedures are now changing and mothers are allowed to keep their babies near them during their stay in hospital and even keep them with them in the bed overnight if they so desire.

Deborah Jackson, a freelance journalist, in her impressively researched rulebook for the thoroughly modern mum, *Three in a Bed*, maintains that for a newborn baby physical 'nearness' to the mother is not enough. She claims that the infant lying in the cot doesn't know that its mother is just across the room from it. She also has no sense of time. According to Jackson, all the baby knows is the pain of isolation if she is not held physically. She advocates sleeping with your baby, and in fact, many mothers of today are doing this with great success. Again, this is a highly controversial area and one that any parent would need to research thoroughly for themselves.

Jean Leidloff is a psychotherapist and author of *The Continuum Concept*. This book is about a society of Yequana Indians where babies are physically connected with their mothers by way of carrying and sleeping with them for as long as the child desires. Leidloff agrees that one of the most significant ways of communicating with the newborn baby is through touch. She finds it incomprehensible that sensible women of the 1990s would go against all of their natural maternal instincts to have their baby physically close to them and treat their baby according to the advice of one solitary male. This is exactly what mothers have done in the past, however, and continue to do in the present. My generation was brought up on Dr Spock. Children of today are brought up on the advice of similar advisers. Some books today still advocate forms of interventionist techniques, such as isolation, as a form of discipline and control of children.

It is unfortunate that such authors constantly look upon a parent's interaction with a child as one like a war between the two desperate parties. When will parents begin to more thoroughly investigate the wealth of information at their fingertips? It seems that some of us entrust the care of our children to the doctors who gain the most exposure on daytime television shows. This is a very sad state of affairs. According to Deborah Jackson:

. . . while a mother is trying to sort her way through all the theories there is a powerful new influence which adds to her confusion:

television. Television feeds her images and tries to sell her things. The sales pitch is often portrayed as professional advice. Child care and consumerism are thus a happy team.

According to some health workers, most inexperienced mothers who are unable to cope with an apparently troublesome baby would rather hear one piece of strong evidence than read five books on the subject and be left to choose on their own.

Parents who are interested in the psychological well-being of their children need to take the first step in investigating the old and the new concepts of child rearing and communication. It is extraordinary that parenting is one of the areas where while there has been a great deal of new knowledge and research, unfortunately this information has not been readily available to parents. As a consequence of this, many of us are still using the antiquated forms of parental communication and parenting skills that both our parents and our grandparents used.

My personal view is that parents should be trained to communicate and parent effectively. They should seek out this information instead of settling for the 'daytime show advice' of people who view children as adversaries to be conquered and speedily disposed of back to their beds where they are kept prisoner by a door handle and a piece of string.

What parents need are practical skills that will solve any problems that arise *and* allow them to maintain a close relationship with their child.

How Did We Learn How to Communicate with Our Children?

If it's true that we begin to learn to communicate prior to our birth, it's no surprise that we find that much of our communication patterns are exactly the same as our parents' communication patterns. How many times have you said something to your child and been shocked by how much it sounded like your own mother or father speaking? It is true that how we learn to parent, and the language that we use to do that, comes largely from imitating our own parents. In many cases, people rebel against their own parent's style of parenting and say 'I'll never do that or say that when I'm a parent'. However, lo and behold, when they become parents, what do they hear coming out of their very own mouths but language patterns from their own childhood experiences. After all, we often buy the same brand of washing powder and toothpaste that our mothers bought when we were children. Why not? They've been tried and true.

If you were to really look at the language that your parents used in parenting you, would you choose to be communicated to in that way once again? I wonder. Most of our parents modelled their language on their parents, who grew up in a society that is very different from the one we know now. The relationship between mothers and fathers was different then as men were the chief breadwinners; society was very different from how it is today and people's beliefs were vastly different from some of the beliefs that we hold today. Even our values are different.

If that's the case, why hasn't our communication style altered along with our changes in society, values and beliefs? Simply because up until recently, we haven't had attention drawn to our communication style. No one has said to us 'Listen to how you're talking, it's so negative. Why not try to change it and see how much better results you'll get and how much better you'll feel'. Scientists who have studied the effect of our language patterns on our attitudes to ourselves have discovered that the language we use is crucial in creating the emotions that we feel. What about the effects of our language patterns upon others? If the language patterns that we use were learned very early on, even as early as in the womb, then the implications of this for expectant parents are highly significant. If we wish to communicate positively with our children and get positive results then maybe we need to alter our communication style.

On one of the Talking with Kids workshops, Rick, a single parent and who had been very quietly taking in all that had been said on the workshop, suddenly spoke up in a discussion regarding the language that we use with children. This is what he said:

> My name is Rick and I'm 40 years old. I have a seven-year-old son whom I love very much and who I only get to see on weekends. I came from a very dysfunctional family. No I wasn't sexually abused. No my parents weren't alcoholics.
>
> Nevertheless I have been struggling for 40 years to recover from the unique kind of abuse that my parents unknowingly carried out upon me. I'm talking about verbal abuse. Verbal abuse is the most insidious kind of emotional abuse and it can scar a child for life. I have worked very hard with my son to ensure that I haven't carried on the language patterning and communication style of my parents. The way that all of you parents are talking to your kids probably seems normal because that's how you were spoken to as a child. But what is normal isn't always right or best. Not only are we talking in negatives when we talk to our kids, but we are talking our kids into roles for their future without even knowing it. Your kids will act according to how you talk to them.

There was stunned silence amongst the group as each parent began to reflect upon how they talk to their children.

Never a truer word was spoken than from this rather reserved man sitting in the corner and observing us all with a keen eye and an even keener ear.

Over the years I have been involved as a teacher on many personal development workshops. It is on these workshops that adults find the words and feelings to express how they feel about themselves and their lives. My observations as a teacher on these courses has shown me that in almost every single adult who has low self-esteem or some area in their life that doesn't work for them, the patterns leading to these pitfalls have emerged from their early childhood years. One of the most significant factors affecting life success and reported by all of these course participants was their verbal and non-verbal communications with their parents. Rick's comment was painfully brought home to me by observing those course participants who were willing to both identify their own areas of communication breakdown and their origins.

The Importance of Language

It is true that we force our children into certain roles within the family or the classroom by the language that we use with them. A child learns to survive in her family or class by playing the role that we have unconsciously assigned to her. A child should have the opportunity to develop and experience various roles so that she can achieve a balance in her life. Maybe then there wouldn't be the need for personal development workshops for adults at all. In families of today there are many little girls who are 'Daddy's princess' and many boys who are 'Mummy's little man'. The role of 'Daddy's princess' can occur when the father's emotional needs aren't met by his wife and he transfers these needs onto his daughter, elevating her to the status of princess. This not only encourages the daughter to demand a great deal of attention, but places a lot of unwanted responsibility upon her as a child. Similarly, the role of 'Mummy's little man' rears its ugly head when the mother's emotional needs are not met within her relationship with her partner and she transfers all of her attention onto her son. The biggest shock of all to parents is when they realise that many of them are even now as grown adults still playing the role of the 'princess' or the 'responsible man' who rescues helpless women.

Let's explore some of the other roles that we may be unwittingly pushing our children into.

'Sandra the saint'

One mother acknowledged her part in creating a saint in her daughter, Sandra, after the group pulled her up on this revealing communication.

> Sandra is just so good, and she always does the right thing. She never has a hair out of place and never talks back to her teachers or to us. She always plays with the same little friends in the playground and at home and always comes in the first top five in her class. We're so lucky to have her. She makes us look less than perfect sometimes and that makes us pull our own socks up, if you know what I mean.

Some children adopt the role of the family saint in their efforts to try to please their parents. This means that they may repress those emotions that are frequently considered to be 'negative': emotions such as anger, fear and jealousy. If we repress all of the negative sides of our personality in a great effort to be liked (and many of us do), we often find that our 'bad side' shows itself in occasional major outbursts that can be very inappropriate. Far better to have a balance in our expression of ourselves than this lopsided persona of the saint.

'Tommy is such a quiet boy'

Here is another comment made by one of our parents that revealed his role for his son.

> Tommy is such a quiet boy. Honestly, sometimes I don't even know he's around.
> He's such an introvert he lives in his own little world. We're lucky because he never gives us any trouble. You know, I've never even seen him once get angry at his brothers or sisters. He always locks himself away in his room and amuses himself. He's never under foot like some kids can be.

Tommy probably learned very early on that his parents were a lot happier when he wasn't around. His parents also may have given him the signal that children should be seen and not heard. The Tommys of this world grow up to be very lonely adults.

'Patty the doer'

Some parents communicate to their children that their only value is in how much they can do, how much they can achieve. This is how 'Patty the doer' is created. Patty's parents' comments were:

> Our Patty is the quiet achiever. She has won numerous medals for swimming and ballet and she always comes first in her class at school. I'm sure that she'll be elected school captain again next year. She's never afraid of hard work. Our Patty's always the first to get the job done. We're so proud of her strong work ethic.

It sounds like poor Patty has very little balance in her life, after all, she spends all of her time out there achieving things so that Mum and Dad will continue to love her.

'Susan the star'

Then there is the case of 'Susan the star'. This is how Susan's parents created her role in life:

> Susan is our little actress. She's incredibly talented, you know! She has such high standards. It's a shame her sisters don't have the same standards. They seem to give her a hard time about being a perfectionist, but we just admire her tremendously. She always stands out in the crowd, you know.

Obviously Susan has quite a lot to live up to. Of course we would all like our children to be stars or heroes. Stars and heroes are so busy trying to shine and stand out that they often miss the fun of the experience they are supposed to be enjoying. Being the star also makes it difficult for them to be a team player as they are so used to being independent and going it alone.

37

Brainwashing Children

Fortunately, all the parents on this particular workshop were very open to accepting feedback about their communications with their children. All could identify at least one role that they were unknowingly steering their child towards. They were all very willing to do something about it and returned the next day eager to learn new strategies for communicating with their children.

We brainwash our children every day without even being aware of it. Scientific research shows that you don't have to put someone into a trance to brainwash them. All you have to do is say the same statement to them often enough and it will go directly into their subconscious mind. Many parents don't realise that there are many natural trance states that occur and therefore many opportunities to be sending positive or negative messages to their child's subconscious mind. If you constantly tell a child that she is clever while she's in a naturally occurring trance state, such as watching television or concentrating on a game, then to the child's subconscious mind this

is a self-fulfilling prophecy. The child will develop a very strong belief that she is clever and she will therefore demonstrate the behaviour of someone who is clever. Simple really, isn't it! Your words can build or bruise, and it's entirely your choice. If you say to a child often enough that she is stupid, she'll believe you. After all, you are bigger and stronger than she is, and you're the grown up, so you *must* be right. She *is* stupid!

Telling your child that she is stupid is a form of direct verbal abuse. It is often open, obvious and direct. These are what I call the 'put downs'.

Some of the more common put downs include telling your child that she's dumb, stupid, ugly or fat and she will never amount to anything. Other direct forms include reminding the child of her previous bad behaviour; humiliating her in front of her friends, siblings, teachers or parents' friends; reinforcing all of her own negative beliefs about herself, that is, kicking her when she's down; and taking delight in the child's suffering.

Some forms of verbal abuse are more subtle and these are indirect abuse. Some of the more common indirect forms of verbal abuse involve the use of humour such as sarcasm and teasing. Some parents do this by jokingly criticising their child in a public place and then later saying that they were only joking. This is a pretty cruel trick to play on any child. No amount of saying that you were joking can make up for this sort of behaviour and it's far more common than we realise.

The most common form of verbal weapon used against children of all ages is that of making judgments. Many parents do this without any awareness of their behaviour. Judging a child is a clever way of controlling her, but it usually results in her feeling dejected, unloved, blamed and discouraged. One way of judging is to belittle a child's experience, thoughts, feelings and achievements. This conveys to the child that her feelings, ideas and behaviour are no good and that she is unworthy. Most children respond to this by withdrawing and not communicating things to their parents for fear of judgment. Finding

39

fault is another form of judgment. Fault-finding parents seem to have the need to constantly point out to the child where she is going wrong and how she 'should' be doing things. This constant criticism is very disempowering.

Many fault-finding parents are themselves perfectionists who have unrealistic expectations of both themselves and of others. Of course, this fault finding can be performed both verbally and non-verbally. Sometimes a disapproving look can substitute for many unkind and unsupportive words. The problem with fault finding is not only does it hurt the child emotionally, it teaches her the behaviour of finding fault constantly in others and at the same time fails to change her poor behaviour. Rather, it reinforces it by focusing only upon the bad behaviours that she performs. Fault finding is damaging for you as parents, as it encourages your child to withdraw from you or to express her fear and anger of you through resentment or aggression.

In summary, I would like to remind you once again that the majority of these direct, indirect, judging and fault-finding forms of communication are learned by modelling our behaviour on that of our own parents. We now have the choice to become aware of the origins of our verbal and non-verbal forms of communication. When we become aware of our behaviours then, and only then, can we start to do something about them. This is not to say that we shouldn't discipline our children or offer them constructive criticism and guidance, far from it. Perhaps in the analysis of our own communication patterns we can find a balance that will allow us to educate, inspire and nurture our children.

In Chapter 4, 'Classic Communication Patterns in Parenting', we will be exploring in depth the various styles of communication common to parenting. As an introduction to this area, why not take the time to analyse some of the less useful forms of communication that you might be using with your child. You can do that by answering the following brief questionnaire. This questionnaire focuses on the styles of communicating that you may be using, rather than giving specific examples. You can use it to look at your own communication patterns and that of significant others in the life of your child. Remember, this is just one way of looking at how it is that we communicate with our children. This particular extract focuses upon forms of verbal abuse. There are many other styles of communicating that you as parents use every day of your lives in communicating with your children.

Questionnaire

Simply circle the word that most represents how often you use a particular style of verbal abuse with your child.

Blaming
    NEVER   SOMETIMES   FREQUENTLY
Fault finding
    NEVER   SOMETIMES   FREQUENTLY
Teasing
    NEVER   SOMETIMES   FREQUENTLY
Humiliating
    NEVER   SOMETIMES   FREQUENTLY
Belittling
    NEVER   SOMETIMES   FREQUENTLY
Sarcasm
    NEVER   SOMETIMES   FREQUENTLY
Put downs
    NEVER   SOMETIMES   FREQUENTLY
Harassing
    NEVER   SOMETIMES   FREQUENTLY

What situations with your child prompt you to use any kind of verbal abuse? How does your child typically respond to your communication? How would you like to alter your communication patterns so that you get a more positive result from your child?

Following are some ingredients that I believe are essential in providing the children in a family with a positive and nurturing environment. All of these ingredients are qualities relating to how it is that we communicate with our children. Look at them and decide for yourself those which you would choose to incorporate in your family environment.

- The overall attitude in the household is a positive one and this is reflected in the language of the family members.
- Family members communicate openly that they care for and will support one another.
- Everyone in the family is encouraged to freely talk about their fears, hopes, dreams and concerns.
- Communication between all family members is honest and congruent as much as is possible and without any hidden agendas.
- Each member of the family is valued for who they are as an individual.
- The parents in the family enjoy their role and do it willingly and not just from a sense of duty.
- The family members enjoy each other's company and don't just get together out of a sense of obligation.
- The children in the family are nurtured and encouraged to develop their own views and their own independence.

So you can see not only is positive nurturing communication necessary prior to birth it is absolutely essential in shaping the lives and attitudes of children of all ages.

Healthy families require healthy communication.

Key Points

❖ The human foetus can see, hear, experience, taste, and learn on a primitive level, *in utero*.

❖ In the 1960s and 1970s, Dr Thomas Verny discovered scientific proof that the unborn child communicates with the mother.

❖ It was concluded that the communication between the mother and the foetus directly affects the future self-esteem and self-concept that the child has of herself. That is to say, the quality of the communication between mother and foetus directly affects the future mental health of the child.

❖ The feelings and actions of the father towards the expectant mother and the child had a significant effect upon the mother's state and therefore the child's state.

❖ Dr Frederick Leboyer believes that the birthing process has a marked effect upon the future psychology of the child.

❖ Dr Henry Truby discovered that the foetus copies the speech patterns of the mother by movement as early as six months *in utero*.

❖ Deborah Jackson and Jean Leidloff consider physical contact with one parent to be crucial to the child's development as a healthy individual.

❖ The style of communication patterns that we use in parenting are set up by our own parents and we tend to copy this style with very little consideration for its effects upon the child.

❖ Many parents are verbally abusing their child without even being aware of it.

CHAPTER THREE

Miscommunication: How Does It Happen?

Miscommunication can occur so easily it's a wonder that any of us have successful and peaceful communications at all. There are times that we do, however, and what we need to look at is what it is that we do when we have one of those successful communications.

Cast your mind back to the last time you had a really successful communication with someone, one that you felt was clear, open and achieved the result that you wanted. Now think of a time when the communication was not successful and you came away feeling angry or confused or frustrated at not achieving your outcome. So what did you do differently in this instance? What was it about this particular communication that made you think that it was unsuccessful? Did you and the other person really listen to one another or were you too busy thinking of how you were going to reply to their comment? Did you have a good rapport with the other person? Did you feel like you were on common ground and talking on the same wavelength? Were you congruent, that is did your thoughts feelings, actions and words all match up to present the truth of what you were saying? Did you approach the conversation with the other person with an open mind or had you already decided there were two points of view — yours and the wrong one? Were you looking for a win–lose outcome (a situation in which one party wins and the other loses because of an unequal power relationship) or a win–win outcome (a situation in which both parties desire a positive and harmonious outcome for each other, and in which there is equal power in the relationship) from the conversation with that person? All of these factors affect whether or not our communication is successful and whether or not we come away from it feeling good about ourselves and the other person.

Let's look more closely at these areas and see if we can highlight some of the reasons why our communications with our children might not be working for us.

Beliefs and Values

One of the major contributing factors to a lack of communication comes from the differences that we experience between our child's beliefs and values and our own beliefs and values. Purely because of the different stages of mental development between us and our child, we would expect that his values would differ from our own. He sees the world through very different eyes from us. His world is characterised by more free time, fewer responsibilities, less seriousness and less focus upon independence than us, depending on the child's age and stage of development.

If you were to imagine some of the beliefs that your child might hold, what would they be? Would some of their beliefs coincide with the following list?

- Adults get to do whatever they want to do.
- Adults can eat whatever they want.
- Children don't get to stay up as late as they want to, but adults do.
- Older kids have more fun.
- School is no fun.
- School is more fun than having to go out to work.
- Mum and Dad have lots of money.
- The smaller you are the more you get picked on.

- Junk food is great.
- Things that happen in the movies come true.

This list could go on and on, but it gives you some idea as to how a child's beliefs may differ from your own. Most of you would agree that these beliefs are significantly different from your own.

Now I'd like you to imagine what your child's five most important values in life might be, no matter their age, and write them down.

No doubt many of these values would differ from your own. You may not put rollerblading, junk food and movies on your priority list. However, have a look and see if there are any common values that both you and your child hold as being important. If so, then you have some common ground to work from. By appealing to your child's values you can motivate him more successfully because he will see clearly the value for him in whatever he is being asked to do. Use your child's highest values to begin to build rapport with him. Talk about the things that are important in his world even if it is very different from those things that you value in your world. Who knows, you might even learn something new!

Establishing Rapport

Establishing rapport simply means building up a relationship between yourself and the child.

Many parents fail to do this because they forget that their child probably has different values from themselves and therefore probably thinks quite differently about things than they do. To build rapport you need to reduce the differences between yourself and your child by trying to find the common ground where your values meet. Then and only then do you have a place to bargain from. Of course, all of this assumes that you are coming to the conversation with an attitude that says you value your child's opinion and respect his values as much as you value and respect your own.

For many parents, this is where the difficulty starts. They think because they are the parents that they have the right to force their values onto the child without considering the child's values at all. Of course, this is always 'for the child's own good'. It's amazing to me that some of us give our friends more respect than we do our own children. We would never even consider treating our best friend with such a lack of respect, so why do we do it to our children? We do it because we have been brought up to believe that children are naturally bad and unless we get control over them they will dominate us, or worse still, turn out to be little monsters. In the cold hard light of day, this is ridiculous. Generations upon generations of parents have learned their parenting skills from modelling their own parents. It is truly unfortunate that as society has changed, parenting skills have not. We may not physically beat our children as much as our grandparents did, but we emotionally beat them instead.

Only when parents start recognising that their children have values and worthwhile opinions too will they be able to adequately build rapport with them, thus removing the age-old power struggle that has existed between parent and child.

When your teenager is telling you something deep and meaningful and you continue to fold the washing or continue to iron the clothes, then that breaks rapport. When your four-year-old is telling you about preschool and you're watching the television and you murmur, 'That's nice, darling', you're breaking rapport. Sometimes we break rapport without even being aware of it. How many times have you actually stopped what you were doing when your child was telling you something and really listened to him? How do you know that what he's about to tell you isn't important? When it comes to children a useful rule to follow is 'Don't assume anything'.

Better to organise a special time for you and your teenager or four-year-old to talk — a time when you can give them your undivided attention and build rapport. For those of you who are thinking that if you did this you'd never get any work done, think about achieving some sort of balance by getting your work done when you need to and organising that other special time to talk and be with your child as well.

Active Listening

Another way in which we break rapport and cause miscommunication is when we not only fail to stop physically and listen, but when we fail to listen actively. 'Active listening' is a technique that many family therapists and psychotherapists use with children to get the children to talk to them. It is a skill that can be acquired by any parent given a little practice. The focus of active listening is to feed back to the child his statement so that you can check that your interpretation of his message is correct. This also gives the child validation that you have truly gotten his message.

Have you ever had a situation where you were telling your partner or a friend something really important and you just knew that they were pretending to listen but in actual fact they just 'weren't there'. Many of us when we listen to someone are busy planning what we are going to say in reply, what advice we are going to give, how we're going to solve their problem for them, instead of really being there for them and listening to them 100 per cent.

This is the trap that most parents fall into because when they listen their way they take on board their child's problem as if it's their own. The effectiveness of the family therapists and psychotherapists with children lies in the fact that they can dissociate from the child's problem, step back from it and see it clearly by using active listening. Of course, this can be quite a challenge when you're a parent. The skill of active listening can be easily learned, but the actual carrying out and practice of it at home is where most parents seem to fall down. Firstly, they have to be really willing to hear their child's point of view. Given the history of parenting in our society, this way of communicating with children hasn't exactly been encouraged.

Second, they must be willing to actually put time and effort into practising the technique. Many of us are so used to fighting time that we're not prepared to try a new approach, even if it might work, because it's better the devil you know than the one you don't. Besides, when you've been doing something one way for many years it becomes a habit and habits don't change overnight.

Active listening as a skill can be acquired with a little effort and a lot of patience. Of course, active listening works both ways and a truly effective way of communicating as a family would be to encourage your children to actively listen to you if you promise to actively listen to them. A true win–win situation.

Below is an example of a parent who hasn't learned to actively listen. Notice that she makes big assumptions about how her child feels and that she tries to immediately 'fix the problem' as opposed to letting the child speak his mind freely.

John: Mum, I hate school. My spelling teacher is a real rat.
Mum: You mustn't say that. Your teachers are all excellent. Are you getting into trouble again? You're probably daydreaming and not listening in class. That's not good enough, John. I've told you before you need to listen to your teachers if you want to do well and get a good job.
John: Yes, Mum.

In this scenario, poor John had barely opened his mouth and his mother jumped on him, making a lot of assumptions, bringing up past history of him getting into trouble at school and doing very little to encourage John to open up to her.

In contrast, let's look at the same scene, but this time one where the mother uses the skills of active listening.

John: Mum, I hate school. My spelling teacher is a real rat.
Mum: So you think that your spelling teacher is a real rat.
John: I sure do. She keeps giving me low marks because my handwriting is bad. I always spell the word right, but she says she takes marks off me because she can't read it properly.
Mum: Is that right. So are you having trouble with your handwriting?
John: Well, sort of. I can print okay, but when we went away on holidays last term they started teaching running writing and I missed out.
Mum: What if I helped you a little each evening with your running writing?
John: Okay, Mum. Maybe then the teacher will have to give me the mark for spelling that I deserve. I guess it's not her fault that I'm having trouble writing. Thanks for helping me, Mum.

In this scenario of active listening, John's mother didn't launch into accusing him of anything or bringing up past history. She encouraged him to open up by paraphrasing what he said so that he knew he'd been heard. That way she got to check that the assumptions that she'd made were correct. Notice how she didn't say, 'Yes you do have bad handwriting. You'll have to put more effort into it, won't you.'

We will be learning the skill of how easy it is to use active listening in Chapter 7, 'A Change for the Better'.

Congruency

A lack of congruency is another major factor affecting rapport and creating miscommunication. Remember in Chapter 1 where I said that children have a built-in radar for anything that even hints of a lack of honesty? Well, in such a situation you are being incongruent, which your child will quickly detect. When what you feel, what you say and what you do all match up, then you are being congruent.

How many times have you said 'yes' when you really wanted to say 'no'? And how many times have you said 'no' when you really wanted to say 'yes'? How many times have you said kind words to your child when you were seething inside? How many times have you pretended to be angry just to get them to listen to you? When we fail to be congruent we affect the rapport that we have built up between ourselves and the other person, because on some level the other person knows that we aren't being totally truthful.

Sensory Modalities Used in Language

The language that we use often favours words from one of our five senses, vision, feeling, sound, smell and taste. Miscommunication can occur because people are operating out of different sensory modalities in the way that they talk. Let me show you what I mean.

The majority of people use words that come from the first three sensory modalities. For example, people who favour a visual modality are often heard saying, 'I see now, or 'Yes, that's clear'. These people love colour and design, and always talk about what they see. People who favour the auditory or sound modality are inclined to love music and the sound of their own voice. They often say, 'That rings a bell' or 'That sounds right' or 'Just tell me one more time'. People who favour a feeling mode often say, 'I get this gut feeling' or 'It just feels right'. Sometimes a person doesn't use language from any of these categories, but instead talks like a computer, using only words that are what I call 'thinking words'. Such a person might say, 'I will analyse the statistics and get back to you'.

Can you imagine what might happen when you put two people together who use the same modality in their language? Well, it's instant rapport. They feel that the other person is on their wavelength and it's like they've been bosom buddies for a lifetime. However, put two people together who favour opposing sensory modalities in their language and you can just imagine the conflict and miscommunication that can occur.

Imagine a scenario where a highly visual person is trying to sell a car to a highly feeling person. The poor car salesman is spending all of his time focusing the client on the coloured brochures and the external effects of the car and all the client is interested in is how does the car feel when he sits in the driver's seat and how does it feel when he takes it for a test drive. Similarly, a salesman who focuses on the feeling aspect of the car with a client who is a thinker will find that the client won't be interested in the feeling of the plushness in the velour-covered seats. All he will want to know is the fuel consumption and details regarding the on-road costs. The sensory modalities that we favour in our language significantly affect our communication and our miscommunication.

So next time you try to get your teenage daughter to wear clothes that look fabulous to you (because you are visual), but aren't comfortable to her (because she's a feeler), watch out. Next time you give your eight-year-old a dictionary for Christmas (because you're a thinker) and all he wanted was a tape recorder (because he's auditory), think again. Remember the differences we have in our values, beliefs and sensory modalities.

Good communication comes from being able to build rapport with your children by appealing to a common value that you both have and talking in the sensory modality that they use.

This all sounds terribly complicated, but when you start actually using it in practice you discover what a fabulous means of communication it is and how much time it saves you in the long run with your children. More of this in Chapter 7, 'A Change for the Better'.

Conflict

Out of miscommunication comes conflict. Many of you may think that I would be opposed to miscommunication, and as a general rule I am, as I believe it creates a great deal of unnecessary stress within the family. A little conflict, however, can occasionally be of benefit in re-establishing the ground rules between parents and children and can in some cases bring the family much closer together. There is something about sorting out your differences that draws people closer. Conflict can open up avenues of change and can provide challenges. When conflict results in miscommunication on a regular basis, both children and parents have been known to exhibit many of the following symptoms: confusion, aggression, withdrawal, loneliness, resentment and stress.

In contrast to this, when the conflict is handled successfully with good communication then both children and parents have been known to exhibit the following symptoms: a sense of fun, power, friendship, peace, a sense of achievement, relaxation and comfort.

The Interior Designer Parent

A significant conflict of interests and resultant miscommunication often occurs when the parents have set a life plan for the child, one that differs from the child's own personal set of values and beliefs. Some parents are like interior decorators; they design their child's life like they are furnishing their home, in intricate detail. Mentally designing every aspect of your child's life can be very dangerous for both you and the child. Interior designer parents carefully control their child's activities and that takes up a lot of time and energy. They choose their child's friends and they can also be heard using a lot of language that includes 'you must', 'you should' and 'you have to'. We all have a tendency to want to control things, but if we do it to extremes then how can we appreciate the unique qualities of our children? When their uniqueness threatens us we step on it and try to make them as much like us as possible. Unwittingly, we try to create little carbon copies of ourselves. Parents often use their power to deny their child's individuality and to force him to go against his own basic beliefs and values. This teaches the child that his beliefs and values don't matter, causing a significant lack of self-esteem.

If this is a pattern that continues in a family then chances are that this child will soon not have any values and opinions of his own. He will be a puppet who can't think for himself. Appreciating a child's uniqueness can allow us to relax more as parents and it certainly reduces our level of stress and frustration.

Even when a child is grown up the interior designer parent likes to choose an appropriate profession for him and even goes so far as to dictate who he will marry. Yet again a dependent child–adult is created who has no true sense of self.

When a child is young he needs direction and structure, but as he approaches the teenage years he needs much more flexibility and more control over his own decision-making.

Growing with Your Child

Another miscommunication pitfall is when parents don't seem to have an appreciation of their child's developmental level. They forget that little Jimmy is no longer a three-year-old and start reminding him to eat his greens, which in turn frustrates the life out of Jimmy (who is 14 years old) who then communicates this in anger and re-sentment, and the cycle of miscommunication continues.

Once a parent becomes aware that she is not treating her child appropriately for his age then she can easily change her behaviour towards the child and good communication is restored. Below are some scenarios that highlight the types of difficulties that parents might have in being aware of their child's developmental level.

> *Tim*: Mum, I really want a boogie board for my birthday. Can I have one this year please? Please, Mum.
>
> *Mum*: But they're dangerous, darling. I can't have my baby out there on those big waves when it's dangerous. You're the only baby that I've got.

Tim is certainly not a baby at 12 years of age and his mother's lack of awareness of his age and the skills that he has is causing Tim a lot of embarrassment with his friends and a lot of built-up resentment against his mum. Tim's mum still sees him as her baby and is relying on this as her criterion for deciding what sort of toys he should have and what sort of activities he should participate in. Yes, it would be dangerous for a baby or a toddler to go out on a boogie board, but a healthy, active 12-year-old boy should be allowed to do activities like boogie boarding and surfing. Tim's mum's lack of awareness of his stage of development brought about some serious miscommunication.

Let's look at another scenario.

Cassie's mother always takes her shopping with her to the supermarket. Cassie is only two and a half and she gets really tired of walking up and down the aisles. Her mother refuses to put her in the trolley and wheel her around because she considers that that is only for babies and Cassie is a 'big girl'. Poor little Cassie gets tired and bored, and then always ends up getting into some mischief such as pulling packets down from the bottom shelf onto the floor. Cassie's mother always gets hysterical when this happens and smacks Cassie, telling her that her behaviour just isn't good enough and that she should be acting like 'a little lady and not a hooligan'.

Cassie's mother obviously has expectations of Cassie that are way beyond what most mothers would expect of a two-year-old. When Cassie goes shopping with her father, she gets to ride in the trolley and help him get things off the shelf at her level. These mixed messages that Cassie receives from both parents causes miscommunication and a great deal of conflict between Cassie's parents. Cassie is confused about what is acceptable behaviour.

In another scenario, Marie's father had promised her something really special for her birthday. Weeks went by and every day she asked her dad what the surprise birthday present was, but he wouldn't tell her. When Marie's birthday came she was so excited. She really hoped that her father had bought her that doll that she'd been asking for for weeks. Marie's father bounded into her room and told her to get all dressed up because they were going out to see a special play. Marie didn't even know what a play was, but when they were in the big theatre and the lights were turned down she found it awfully difficult to keep still. Daddy kept glaring at her and telling her to keep still, but the play seemed to go on for hours and hours.

On the way home in the car, Marie began to cry. It was the worst birthday that she had ever had. She really wished that her father had bought her that doll instead of taking her to that dumb old play.

Marie's father didn't realise that taking a five-year-old to see the play *Hamlet* was inappropriate. He just thought that the things that excited him about the theatre would also excite her. He certainly learned otherwise.

Many parents perceive their children as either younger than they are or older than they are. Below are some ideas that I believe are useful in acquainting yourself with the developmental level of your children.

The first thing to do is to take a long hard look at your child. Compared to children two or three years younger than him how does your child compare in terms of physical maturation, the way he thinks, the games he likes to play and the sort of activities that he prefers to be involved in? Also compare how he interacts with others and the types of things that he is learning at his particular stage of schooling. If you can't easily make this comparison then get your child together with some younger children and observe them over a period of time. Watch and listen to the differences between them as they talk, play and interact together.

Now get a photo of your child from a few years ago and observe how much he has changed physically. Try to remember how he played, talked and interacted back then and compare it to how he functions in the world now.

Next compare your child to a couple of children that are two or three years older than he is. Compare them in exactly the same way as you did with the younger children. Notice the things that separate your child from the babyish world of those younger years and also the things that separate him from the adult world. This will help you orient in your mind your child's particular stage of development. By developing an awareness of who your child is you will more than likely start to respond to him appropriately for his age.

By merely spending some time in your child's world without any particular outcome in mind — for example, just going for a walk together — you will gather important information that will stand you in good stead in terms of achieving successful communications with your child.

A useful thing to do is to write down some of the goals that you find you are expecting your child to be achieving at this point in time. What kinds of behavioural standards are you setting for your child? What are you expecting from your child right now at this point in time? Do your expectations match up to your child's developmental level or are your expectations inappropriate for the level that your child is at home?

When we build rapport with our children by appealing to their values, appreciating their beliefs, acknowledging their developmental level and actively listening to them using their individual sensory modality, we open the door for a close relationship and clear communication to occur.

Key Points

❖ Look closely at what you think, feel, say and do when you have *successful* communication with someone.

❖ Look closely at what you think, feel, say and do when you have an *unsuccessful* communication with someone.

❖ Miscommunication can occur due to differences between your beliefs and values and your child's beliefs and values.

❖ Rapport is built when you reduce the differences between yourself and your child.

❖ You can build rapport with your child by appealing to his values and accepting that his beliefs may be different from your own.

❖ Active listening is an excellent means of building rapport and maintaining it.

❖ By using active listening, you will be encouraging your child to talk with you about himself.

❖ Active listening is a skill that can be learned by any individual given a willingness to learn, a little effort, a little time and a lot of patience.

❖ Active listening helps you to step back and look clearly at your child's problems. By stepping back you are more effective in the help that you can give.

- ❖ Congruency occurs when what you think, feel, say and do all match up.
- ❖ The language that we use often favours words from the three major sensory modalities: to feel, to see and to hear.
- ❖ You can build rapport with your child by talking in his individual sensory modality. We will learn to do this in Chapter 7.
- ❖ Conflict can open up avenues of change and can provide challenge.
- ❖ Conflict handled successfully can result in a sense of fun, power, friendship, peace, achievement, relaxation and comfort.
- ❖ Major conflict and miscommunication can occur when a child's parents have a set life plan for him that conflicts with his own set of beliefs and values.
- ❖ Miscommunication can be avoided by becoming more aware of your child's developmental level.
- ❖ When we build rapport with our children by appealing to their values, appreciating their beliefs, acknowledging their developmental level and actively listening using their individual sensory modality, we open the door for a close relationship and clear communication to occur.

CHAPTER FOUR

Classic Communication Patterns in Parenting

In Chapter 2, 'When Does Communication Begin?', we had a taste of some of the styles we use to communicate with our children. In this chapter we will be exploring these styles in much greater depth. In order to understand some of the classic communication patterns in parenting we first need to explore our reasons for becoming parents and also some of the myths that surround parenting. Both of these areas have significant effects upon the communication style that we use with our children.

Let's begin by asking a fairly confronting question: Why did you become a parent? We all have our own reasons for wanting to have children. Here are just some of the reasons that the parents in one of my workshops gave for becoming parents. It was interesting to note that in many of the couples in the group the husband and the wife had very different reasons for wanting to have children.

- I wanted to make my own mother happy. She so desperately wanted to be a grandmother.
- I thought that having a child would make me feel fulfilled as a person.
- Becoming a father was important to me because I wanted a son to carry on my name.
- My own family background was abusive and I thought that maybe I could fix that by creating my own happy family.

- Kids keep you young at heart.
- I want a child to look just like me.
- I want to teach a child about the joys of life.
- I want a baby so that he'll be there for me when I get old and need looking after.

From my own experience with participants in my workshops it seems that the reasons for wanting to become a parent fall into four major categories: love, ego, compensation and approval.

Love, Ego, Compensation and Approval

Let's examine *love* motives first.

People who want to become parents because they are motivated by love generally express similar concerns. They want to give love and affection so that they can help a child grow and develop, and to contribute to that child's knowledge of life and her general happiness. This is neither a good or bad reason for wanting to become a parent. In view of the task that parenting presents to us, however, this choice is probably the most useful one for both the parent and the child.

Now let's look at *ego* reasons for becoming a parent.

In this point of view it seems that the parent is out for something for themselves, something that may be a deficit need from their own childhood. This is probably not a very useful place to come from as, inevitably, the parents will be disappointed if the child doesn't measure up to expectations. These parents usually express the desire to have someone around who will think that they're the greatest. The child is used as a means of gratifying the parents' ego whether it be to inherit the family fortune, fulfil the parents' dreams of success in a chosen field of expertise, or to prove that the parents can do something well.

Some of us become parents to *compensate* for the lack of happiness in either our work situation or in our marriage or because we have few friends socially. We may even be compensating for the lack of happiness that we had in our own childhood experience of family. Compensation is not a very useful reason for parenting.

Let's look at *approval*.

Many of us choose to become parents to gain the approval of others. We may do it to gain the approval of our parents, our friends, our co-workers or other relatives and not because we want to become parents to love and nurture.

All of these reasons for wanting to become parents feature significantly in how we communicate with our children once we become parents. For example, if you are a parent who is compensating for a lonely married life you may focus all of your attention onto the child and expect her to play the role of spouse for you emotionally. If you're someone who has had children to carry on the family name, then your communications will undoubtedly focus around the child's responsibility in doing this task. For those parents who had children to please their own parents it may be a case of verbal abuse involving accusations such as 'I don't know why I ever had you kids!' When adults want to parent out of a desire to nurture and love and educate their children, then it follows that the outcome and style of their communications with the child will be to nurture, love and educate.

Examining the reasons we had for becoming parents or examining our reasons for wanting to become parents in the future is very significant in its implication for communication style and effectiveness.

Now I'd like you to explore your own reasons for becoming parents or for wanting to become parents in the future. Think about this carefully and then write down your thoughts.

No matter what your reasons for becoming a parent, whether they are useful reasons or not, our focus should now fall onto 'How can I use this knowledge to improve how I communicate with my children? Whatever my reasons were, with the knowledge that I now have I can change my communications to ones that nurture, support and educate the child for her own sake to the point where she is a healthy independent individual'. We will be looking very closely in Chapter 8, 'How to Communicate Values to Your Children', at how to achieve this. For the time being it is sufficient to know what you know now, and to at least commit to changing the way you communicate to your children — for example, learning to be aware of your use of any negative language. So let's move on.

Myths of Parenthood

There are a multitude of myths that surround being a parent and these myths affect how it is that we communicate with our children. If you check your own parental beliefs and expectations you may find that you've fallen victim to a parenting myth. Parents who live by these myths often experience disillusionment and discouragement. They get tied in knots because they can't live up to the ideals they have set for themselves, ideals that are based upon myth.

Let's look at some of the more common ones experienced by adults on the Talking with Kids workshops. The first myth that was common to nearly all of the parents that have gone through the program is that of 'total parental involvement'.

Many parents believe that they have to be totally involved in being a parent, to the exclusion of all else. This is crazy. It means that the child is the centre of attention every moment of the day, which is not only unhealthy for the child but unhealthy for the parent. The parent becomes so overinvolved in their child's life they give up their own activities and then can become very resentful of doing so. Parents who do this make statements to their children such as 'How can you do this, after all I've done for you', 'Look at all of the things I've given up for you' and 'I only did it for your benefit'.

Sometimes the parent's communication will express martyrdom or guilt to control the child: 'I'll give up my outing with my friends

for you, it doesn't really matter'.

Overinvolved parents give so much to their children that they prevent their children from learning to take responsibility for themselves and for their own needs. How will these children then function as adults?

These parents take on so much for their children's activities and forget their own activities, thus creating a severe imbalance in their lives. This type of parent makes herself completely indispensable to the child. She will often feel exhausted and trapped as she goes through a vicious cycle of doing too much, becoming exhausted, accepting help from others, and then feeling guilty because she is not fulfilling the parental role alone and without extra support. It seems that overinvolvement can lead you down the path of frustration and burnout. If you don't take time to refuel your own tank you can end up with nothing more to give. Your attitude to parenting could easily turn from joy to disappointment if you take the path of overinvolvement.

Two parents on our Talking with Kids program had this to say about their level of overinvolvement.

We drag ourselves from football match to netball training to scouts to tennis lessons and then to piano lessons. We haven't had any time for ourselves in months. Something has to give and lately it's been our tempers. What can we do?

No matter if you're the parents of teenagers, school-aged children or toddlers, you run the risk of burnout if you get on the vicious overinvolvement cycle. Some tips for spotting whether you have fallen into this parental myth trap have arisen from our workshops. They are as follows:

- Do you always tidy your child's room for her?
- Do you only let your children play with the friends that you select for them?
- Do you do things for your child that she's easily capable of doing for herself?
- Do you give your child no household chores to do?
- Do you do your child's homework for her?

This overinvolvement myth results in a child being so smothered that she may either withdraw or rebel, resist or submit. This pattern of parenting definitely does not empower the child towards independence.

Another popular myth among parents is the absolute 'I have to enjoy being a parent' myth.

No one is going to enjoy every single aspect of parenthood. We all at some time or another want to say, 'Stop the merry-go-round I want to get off'. This is because of the incredible demands that being a parent places upon us. This is especially noticeable in the working woman who gives up her career, to which her self-esteem and identity are linked, to tread the path of motherhood. Here she has little experience and she may be constantly watched by mother and mother-in-law as she travels blindly along the path of selflessness and giving. For men, too, fatherhood is a huge challenge, demanding upon their time and energy. And especially so in the 1990s, where men are now joining in with the housework and childcare responsibilities often after having also done a full day's work themselves.

Two of our Talking with Kids graduates had this to say about their myth of parental enjoyment:

> We feel like such failures. We should be enjoying our time as parents. They grow up so quickly and then all of a sudden they're gone. I don't understand why it's become such a chore. We used to love being parents when they were little. We must be doing something wrong.

The biggest myth of all is the one that reads 'I am responsible for my child's success or failure'.

I often hear parents on my workshops saying such things as, 'Where did we go wrong?' or 'We must have done something wrong' or 'I should have spent more time, taken more care'. This is what one couple had to say about their children:

> We are so disappointed in our children. We really thought that Johnny would come into the family business, instead he wants to be a rock star and go on tour all over the world and Caroline couldn't care less about being a nurse like her mother. All Caroline wants to do is design buildings. She's planning to become an architect. I really thought that we had more influence over them than that. It's such a pity to see them throw their lives away on futile careers. We wanted so much more for them.

The truth is that despite the best of plans our children are not always going to take a path that we have chosen for them. They are not always going to follow in our career paths or be the success that we hope for.

If you think back to Chapter 1 where we looked at our beliefs about parenthood, you may discover that some of your parental myths are expressed in these beliefs. Take the time now to go back and check if you have expressed any of these myths in your belief list. Now is the time to reassess those parental beliefs and prevent burnout, disillusionment and dissatisfaction with parenthood. Instead, you can have healthy beliefs that are realistic and lead to a balanced lifestyle for both yourself and your children.

Classic Communication Styles

Now that we've addressed our reasons for becoming parents and our beliefs about parenting, let's look at some classic styles of communication used in parenting. Each of these styles of communication arise from certain parental myths and belief systems. I wonder if you can identify the beliefs and the myths as I outline the styles most commonly used.

Outcome Styles

The first method and by far the most common today is the win–lose approach where the parent sees any conflict as an opportunity to use her power over the child and to dominate the child, thus winning. This creates out-and-out war between children and their parents. There is the notion that this win–lose approach must start from birth and that you have to let the child know who's boss from the very start. The fear here is that the child may dominate the parent and make the parent look foolish, or worse still, out of control. The child may also take advantage of the parent and therefore abuse her unless she keeps a strong control. Children in families where the win–lose approach is used know full well that there is no point in even expressing their opinion as the parent will always 'win'. Below are some examples of the win–lose type of outcome.

Mum: Trish, come here and put some suntan lotion on. You'll shrivel up like an old woman if you don't.
Trish: I don't need it. I never get burnt. Besides I'm sitting under the umbrella, aren't I?
Mum: You can still get burnt under the umbrella because you've got fair skin. Don't argue with me, young lady. Do as you're told or I'll take us all home.
Trish: Gee, Mum. That isn't fair.
Mum: I won't tell you again. Put that cream on now, do you hear me?

As you can see, the conflict has arisen over whether Trish should put on suntan cream or not. The mother begins by using subtle manipulation and then finishes with the use of power and authority that involves threats. The outcome is that the parent wins and the child loses. I prefer to call this the lose–lose outcome as it seems to me that neither party truly wins in the long term.

Here is another example:

Mum: Steven, I want you to feed the dog. It's your turn.
Steven: Oh! It's not fair. How come I have to do everything around here? Jodie never has to do anything. It's not fair. She can feed the dog. I don't want to. It's her turn.
Mum: Steven you feed that dog now or I'll go and ring up your father and tell him how irresponsible you're being. Do you hear me?
Steven: You always threaten me with that. I hate it (*beginning to get the dog food ready*). I always have to do everything around here. I can't wait till I can move out and get away from this place.

In this example, it's clear that Steven feels resentful about having to do his chores. His mother immediately steps in to use threats. The father is used as the bad guy in this case, which is not very useful for building rapport between father and son. Steven's comments at the end as he submits to the threats indicate his sadness and disappointment at not really being given a chance to defend his side of the story. In actual fact, it was Jodie's turn to feed the dog, not Steven's, but his mother didn't give him the chance to tell her this.

Another popular style of communicating is the lose–win situation which goes something like this.

The child wins by using her power over the parent and the parent gives in to the child's power. In the case of Trish and the suntan cream the scenario would go something like this:

Mum: Trish, I think you should put some suntan lotion on.
Trish: I don't want to. I don't need to.
Mum: Well, I still think that you should because you're so fair-skinned.
Trish: Mum, you don't know anything. I never get burnt. Stop picking on me or I'll tell Dad.
Mum: Oh, I give up. I don't want to argue with you any more. You win.

In this instance, the mother surrendered in the face of Trish's threats. Here is another example:

Dad: Josh. Josh. I'm really busy today doing my tax return. Could you look after the twins for me for just an hour? I promise that it won't be more than an hour.
Josh: Gee, Dad. I was going rollerblading with the guys in about 10 minutes.
Dad: Could you cancel it or make it a bit later? I really need to get this done so that we have some money coming back in next month. I'm relying on my rebate to buy you kids birthday presents next month.
Josh: No. I don't want to cancel the guys. The twins will be okay on their own. Just give them a video to watch.
Dad: No. They really need to be supervised while Mum's out shopping. I'll be in the study concentrating and I won't know

what they're getting up to. I need you to do this.

Josh: Gee. Dad. The guys will really think that I let them down. They'll think I'm a sissy looking after my baby sisters. I can't do it. Not today.

Dad: Can't you see how important it is that this gets done today? It has to be in the mail tomorrow or I could be in real strife.

Josh: Sorry, Dad. No go.

Dad: Well, I guess I haven't given you much notice. Hanging out with your friends probably is more important than my problems.

Of course, the father in this instance did spend a lot of time explaining the importance of his predicament, however, he gave in at the end. He allowed his son to feel that his activities were more important than his father's problems. In this instance, the son definitely won and the father definitely lost. Surely they could have come to some mutual agreement.

In both the win–lose and the lose–win style, the outcome is the same. Both people want their own way and one person tries to convince the other person that they are right, thus winning control.

In both methods, one person goes away feeling defeated and powerless. Parents who employ the win–lose approach usually defend it by saying that it is the quickest way to get things done. From my experience of observing parents employing this method, however, they seem to spend a great deal of time nagging, reminding and prodding the unwilling child to carry out the task and in so doing use more energy and time. These parents suffer the anger, frustration and resentment of their children, who carry out the task often slowly, begrudgingly and definitely not willingly. This style turns joy and love into anger and resentment.

The lose–win method is also useless in that the children usually get their way and they very quickly learn to throw tantrums, control their parents by manipulation and become wild, uncontrollable children who are selfish and who lack insight into their own behaviour. This is not useful in encouraging the child to take responsibility for her actions or to respect others and their property. Due to the fact that these children are so used to getting their own way they extend this to other contexts outside the home, such as their interactions with other children and with teachers at school. It is no wonder that the child who uses this method often feels unpopular, even unloved, because she creates feelings of resentment and anger in her parents. It must be very sad for parents to raise a child whose company they can't stand and who they find it difficult to love.

The big difficulty in families is that often one parent will use the win–lose method and the other parent will use the lose–win method, thereby creating even more conflict, confusion and inconsistency. Some parents start out using a win–lose approach and then eventually give in and use the lose–win approach. Some parents do the reverse. In some families, two different methods are used to communicate with the first- and second-born child, causing one child to feel as though the parents favour her brother or sister.

Most parents get locked into using one method or both because they know of no alternative method that truly works. This is the ultimate parent trap. In thinking now of your preferred method of communicating with your children, write down which if any of these methods you use in your daily life and with whom you use them.

- Win–lose
- Lose–win
- A combination of win–lose and lose–win.

In Chapter 7, 'A Change for the Better', we will be looking in detail at the preferred style of communication that results in a positive outcome for all parties concerned: the win–win approach. But first let's get another slant on the styles of communication most commonly used between children and parents.

Action style

If we take the win–lose approach we can overlay on that another paradigm which looks at the style of action involved, that is to say, the action that the child takes as a result of the parent's win–lose approach. The outcome of this style is that the child *submits* to the parent's will. If we overlay the lose–win approach onto this paradigm we can see that in this case the child *resists* the parent's will. This is the child's action.

In most areas of our lives, we either submit or resist depending upon the context and the individuals involved. In Chapter 7, when we explore the win–win approach, you will discover that the use of this approach means that the style of action is one of neither resistance nor submission, but rather that the individual flows with the course of events. This flowing leads to far less energy being wasted and a greater sense of well-being and cooperation for all concerned.

Another way of looking at the classic styles we use to communicate is to look at the non-verbal side of our communication. In other words, what does our body language reveal about our beliefs, our desired outcomes and our actions. In Chapter 1 remember that I made the point that the non-verbal communication we use is by far the most important side of our communication. A gesture can signify a thousand words. Unfortunately much of our non-verbal communication as parents falls into four negative categories, in that when we use this form of communication with our children we create frustration, distance and a lack of rapport.

The first non-verbal style of communication is the *accuser* body stance. The parent who uses this style also falls into using a win–lose outcome and a style of action that resists his child's point of view. This parent often stands with one hand on his hip, pointing and waving an accusing finger at the child. The verbal side of this action of course is that of verbal abuse, the type we talked about in Chapter 2, 'When Does Communication Begin?'.

This parent's body usually is held very tight and his bottom-line belief is that no one, including his children, cares about him so he needs to yell and shout and blame his children, otherwise his children would not take any notice of him. This is the bully parent who only feels safe when he's fully in control of the situation.

For example, if verbals were put to the non-verbal actions this is what the accuser might say as he wags his finger at his children:

Dad: Haven't I told you selfish little brats a million times to turn that television down when I'm on the phone. What are you, stupid?
Julie and Mark: Sorry, Dad.
Dad: Well sorry isn't good enough. You really take after your mother in the brains department. Everything that goes wrong around here is your fault. I don't know why I ever bothered having you kids. You're more trouble than you're worth.
Julie and Mark: Yes, Dad.

The second rather popular non-verbal stance is the one that I call the *victim*. This parent always chooses an outcome of lose–win and uses an action style of submitting to her children. This parent often displays a worried frown and pleading gestures, such as extending the arms, which says 'I'm sorry'. Her body language is so submissive that if she were a dog this parent would roll over and play dead — at the request of her children, of course. The bottom-line belief of this parent is that she needs to be loved by others to justify her existence. She is continually trying to please her children and failing in the effort. Her children step all over her and consider her a wimp.

For example, if the victim parent were standing there apologetically the scenario might go something like this:

Mum: Tracy, sweetheart. Don't pull your baby brother's hair. He doesn't like it.
Tracy: (*continuing to pull her brother's hair*) Choo, choo. He's a train.

Mum: Now darling. Timmy isn't a train and pulling his hair must hurt him.

Tracy: Choo, choo. This is fun.

Mum: Oh, Tracy! What am I going to do with you? You're such a scallywag. I'm sorry to keep nagging you, darling, but I really think you should let go of Timmy's hair. There's a good girl. Mummy's sorry for spoiling your fun.

The third non-verbal type is the *drama queen* or *drama king*. These parents do anything to get attention, including waving their arms around to distract their children. This parent resorts to an outcome where their child submits to them, but instead of submitting due to force they submit due to manipulation. These parents have a basic belief that they are unlovable and they need constant reminding and reinforcement from their children that they are needed. This need justifies their existence as parents.

The verbal side of this scenario would go something like this as the parent waves her hands around in hysteria.

Mum: Oh my God, Rick! Get down from that tree. You'll fall and break your neck and then you'll have to go to hospital and God knows what I'll do then. You'll be the death of me. Now get down right now.

Rick: But Mum, I'm being really careful and besides I've climbed heaps of trees before.

Mum: Not when I'm around you don't. Oh my God, I can just see that branch giving way and you crashing to the ground. What will I do then?

The fourth non-verbal type is the *reasoner*. This parent is the epitome of cool, calm and collected. Nothing fazes them and they display very little emotion, if any at all. Their body language consists of standing with their arms crossed in a defensive pose which means that they show to their children that they are not vulnerable. The reasoner parents also have a basic belief that they are unlovable. Their outcome is to get their child to submit and they do it not through authority but through reason. They accept no other opinion other than their own because theirs 'makes the most sense'.

The reasoner's stance may be a hand up to the face in deep thought as he proclaims this result to his child:

Dad: I've looked at all of the details calmly and it seems to me that you're not working hard enough in maths. Ninety-three per cent is just not good enough. I'm hiring a maths coach for you next term. I've looked at the nights that you have free and it seems to me that you should give up soccer because your maths is far more important.

Charlie: Can't I do it another night, Dad? The team is really relying on me this season.

Dad: No, I'm afraid that this is the most sensible conclusion. You need to realise the value of mathematics and this is the best way of getting the message home to you. I don't wish to discuss it any further. You start maths coaching on Monday.

If you were to look for your particular style of communication, whether it be the reasoner, blamer, victim or drama queen, you would probably find that you use a combination of these styles depending on the context and the person with whom you are communicating. Nevertheless, there will be a tendency to favour one particular style with each child you communicate with.

Write down now any BFOs (blinding flashes of the obvious) that you have regarding the style of communication that you use non-verbally.

Which do you think is the most effective style for getting your child to turn off the television, for example? Which style do you think would create most stress in your life? Which, if any, are truly effective means of communicating and relating to others? Which style gets results and maintains rapport with the person being communicated with?

Record your results and thoughts now.

Classic Verbal Styles of Communicating

Sensory-based language

Each of us processes information through our senses as was outlined in Chapter 3, 'Miscommunication: How Does it Happen?'. The senses are taste, smell, sight, sound and touch. We tend to favour one or other of the three major senses: sight, sound and touch, as well as the thinking sense, when we communicate with others. This, too, is a classic style of communicating. Have you ever noticed what sensory mode your partner uses when she talks to you, and what about your children? What about you? Do you favour the visual, auditory, feeling or thinking mode? Interesting, isn't it, how we can all be so different.

Below are some scenarios. See if you can tell whether the parent is talking visually, auditorially, in thinking mode or in feeling mode.

Mum: We're going to go shopping now, Angie. My, you look great in that dress. The colour is wonderful. I'm lucky to have such a smart-looking daughter, aren't I? Look, the first thing that I want to do when we get there is have a good browse around and look at everything before we make any decisions. That's how I usually do it, you see. Look first thoroughly and then buy. What do you think?

Angie: Well, Mum. I usually like to try things on before I make a decision. I want to make sure that I get something that's comfortable.

Mum: Well, that's okay. I'll look through and pick things out for you and then you can try them all on, okay?

Angie: Okay, Mum. As long as I get some say in what you choose for me.

Dad: You know, Justin, I've been thinking. This idea of the billycart really isn't very practical. You could get better value for your money if you bought one instead of buying the equipment and building it yourself.

Justin: But Dad, half the fun is in me building it with my friends.

Dad: I understand that and I do want to be reasonable, but it doesn't weigh up to be cost-effective that way. I think you should just buy one.

Mum: I feel so tired after that gym class. I really could do with a massage, but I can't afford it.

Dad: Why don't you sit down here and just relax and listen to the music.

Mum: No. I think I'd feel much better if I had a long hot bath. My muscles are beginning to tighten up already. I can just feel that warm water on my skin.

Dad: It sure sounds good. I'll run the bath for you and I'll turn the music up so you can hear it, too.

David: Wow, that sounds like a great idea, Mum. Can I go and choose the band. I can't wait to tell my friends. This sounds great, Mum. Thanks.

Mum: Well, it's not every day that I see my son turn 18.

David: Cool. I can't wait to hear what Jane's going to say when I tell her that we're having a band. I'm going to go ring her now.

The power of words

Our words have much greater impact than we think. Words can be very emotive, that is to say, they trigger very strong emotions in us depending upon the choice of word employed. So it is in our best interests to become aware of the words that we use, to self-monitor our use of language. When we become good at this and we can identify what language we frequently use, then and only then, can we begin to alter our verbal language patterns to ones that might be more useful and far more effective.

'I' statements

Many of us avoid making statements with the word 'I' because it draws attention to us. Sometimes it's because of old conditioning as a child where we were told not to talk about ourselves all the time and that saying 'I' was showing off. However, the use of 'I' is fantastic because it involves us taking full responsibility for ourselves. It means that we really own what we are saying. We aren't passing the buck and we are very clear in our communications.

See how clear the communication is between this father and daughter when they use 'I' statements:

Dad: I know that you feel that you're old enough to make your own decisions, but the fact is that when you come home late I sit here and worry and I feel just awful. I can't sleep until I know that you're home safe and sound.

Daughter: I do feel like I'm old enough to make my own decisions. Sometimes I'm having so much fun that I lose track of time. It's not that I want you to worry. I guess I never realised how me being late makes you feel. I feel awful that you have to wait up for me and don't get your sleep. Why don't I take the responsibility of ringing you next time I'm going to be late?

Dad: I would appreciate that. I'd feel a lot more comfortable knowing what time you'll be arriving home.

'You' statements

When used in clear commands like 'You are the one that I care about', the use of 'you' is not misleading. However, when 'you' isn't used clearly, it can be misunderstood and interpreted as an accusation; for example, 'You did it'.

In this example, the 'you' statements could be interpreted as accusing and belittling:

Dad: No. Can't you see? You've done it all wrong. What you should do is ring them up first and let them know that you want to have a meeting with them.

Maggie: Dad, you don't understand. I wanted it to be a surprise.

Dad: Well, you kids today always think you know best. You do what you want, but I know you won't get them to agree unless you ring them up first.

'Should' statements

'Should' is the word used to imply that something is wrong with you, that you have done it all wrong and that you can't make decisions for yourself: 'You should have done this instead'. It is also used to place restrictions upon ourselves: 'I want the cake but I should eat the carrot instead'. Hearing yourself use the 'should' word is a tip-off that there's a struggle going on inside you between the part that wants one thing and another part that wants another thing.

Sometimes it's useful to separate the two parts and consider each one separately. For example, 'The cake has yummy icing and I have been good with my diet so far' and 'The carrot is much better for me and I won't feel the least bit guilty after eating it'. When you look at them separately it seems much simpler to make a decision.

I often catch myself 'shoulding' on myself with my self-talk, that is, the talk that goes on inside my head.

Here is an example of how I do that:

> I should have known they'd be late. I should have cooked something that wouldn't spoil. Why don't I ever learn from my mistakes. I should have known they'd be late. They've always been late before. I should have checked with them first to see if they could get here easily. A great host I am.

In this scenario, the guests are running late and the dinner is getting overcooked. I decide to blame myself for their being late and seem to feel that it's my responsibility to get them there on time. In fact, it's not my responsibility and I have no justification for 'shoulding' on myself.

'Yes' and 'no' and 'don't' statements

Often we fail to make our yes and no signals clear. Sometimes we say, 'Yes, but . . .' or 'No, but maybe . . .'. Sometimes we say 'yes' automatically to things that people ask of us without even thinking about them first. Many of us say 'yes' when we really mean 'no'. Most adults spend their parenthood saying 'No, no, no, no, no', or 'Don't' a million times a day. Don't touch, don't do that, don't say that, don't wear that, don't look like that. Parents can find themselves living in a 'don't world' if they're not too careful.

Look at this scenario of a mother and child in a playground.

Mum: Janie, don't swing too high, you might fall off. And don't decide to climb those monkey bars. Little girls shouldn't swing from bars. It's not ladylike. Don't get yourself all dirty. Don't forget we have to go visit Grandma after this. No girl of mine is going to look a ruffian when she visits her grandma. Watch out for the grease on the seesaw. I don't want you getting it down your dress.

Positive and negative focus

One way of looking at our language as parents and educators of children is to look and see if the majority of our use of language falls into the category of positive statements or if it falls into the category of negative statements. Unfortunately, because the history of parenting in our country has been based upon the belief that children are second best, should be seen and not heard, and should always obey their parents without the slightest hesitation, it's no wonder that the majority of us grew up receiving negative statements from our parents. In addition, the evil of the fathers shall be visited upon the sons. We self-perpetuate the cycle of what Alice Miller calls the 'poisonous pedagogy'. In her book, *For Your Own Good*, Miller argues that control of emotions and desires and the exaltation of such values as orderliness and cleanliness above all else is a form of violence that violates the rights of children. John Bradshaw, American author and a leading figure in the field of recovery of dysfunctional families, links Miller's notion of poisonous pedagogy to old beliefs about the behaviour of 'better' children, such as 'children should be seen and not heard' or 'children should not speak until they are spoken to'.

Read the following selection of scenarios and see if any of them ring true for you:

Caitlin: Mummy, Katie isn't playing with me any more.
Mummy: Well, she's being mean. Just you ignore her. You can't trust anyone, you know. Making friends isn't easy. It's hard to find someone that you get on with.

In fact, there could have been any number of reasons why Katie wasn't playing with Caitlin. Without asking any questions, her mother blurted out, within five simple statements, most of her negative beliefs about how life is a struggle and how it's important not to trust others.

Dad: You know you kids make my life a misery. I spend all my time at work, slaving away so you can have rollerblades and skiing holidays and I never get any thanks from you kids. Never.
Kids: Dad, of course we appreciate what you do. We know how hard you work. But we work hard, too. I do all my chores right on time, no questions asked, don't I? And Trish does hers, too, and we've both got lots of homework each night.
Dad: Those were the days when all I had to worry about were homework and household chores. God knows how long you're going to keep up the chores, though. I bet you slacken off as soon as I let up on you. I've got to have eyes in the back of my head to keep you guys doing anything.

This father sure has some difficulty in listening to his kids. All he can focus on is how hard done by he is. He doesn't even notice the evidence of the chores that his children carry out without any complaints. One wonders how long they will continue to be positive in their outlook when their father is so negative in his.

Here are some positive parenting scenarios:

Caitlin: Mummy, Katie isn't playing with me any more.
Mum: How does that make you feel?
Caitlin: Kind of sad. Her mum is too busy to let her play today.
Mum: Would you like to play with me instead? We girls could

have a lot of fun with the Lego in the sunroom. What do you think?

Caitlin: That would be fun, Mummy.

Mum: Great. Well, I just have to spend about twenty more minutes on the ironing and then I'm all yours. Can you help me with the hankies while we're waiting? That way we might even finish sooner.

Caitlin: Okay, Mummy. I like doing the hankies the best.

Dad: You know, I think I need a little more help around here. If you guys pitch in a little more then it would make my life so much easier. I really like being able to buy you kids things and taking you on skiing trips, but to do that I need to get my work done and not have to worry so much about all the chores around the house getting done.

Kids: Dad, of course we appreciate what you do. We do all our chores around the house, no questions asked. We still get our homework done, too.

Dad: Yeah. I guess I hadn't noticed just how much you kids do around here. Maybe we can pool our resources and have two people on one chore so that we all get our chores done sooner. That will give us more time for my work and your homework. What do you say?

Next time you're talking with your children, just go ahead and notice how many 'yes', 'no' and 'should' statements you make. Notice, too, if the majority of your statements to your children are positive or negative. This little experiment can be quite revealing. The answer lies in monitoring the language that you use and then very gradually changing it to language that is more useful and effective. Then and only then can we remove some of the verbal abuse that has existed in the past in communicating with children. In Chapter 7, 'A Change for the Better', we will be discussing how this can be done easily and effectively. But for now, let's look at what might get in our way of making the changes that we want in our communication skills.

Key Points

❖ Our reasons for becoming parents and some of the myths surrounding parenting itself have significant effects upon the style of communicating that we use with our children.

❖ Our reasons for wanting to become a parent can fall into four major categories: the desire to love, the need to fulfil the ego, the desire for approval and to compensate for unmet needs left over from our childhood.

❖ Some of the more common myths about parenting include:
 — you have to be totally involved in being a parent to the exclusion of all else
 — you are responsible for your child's success or failure.

❖ Some of the most classic styles of communicating that we use in our parenting include:
 — win–lose approach
 — lose–win approach
 — a combination of the above two approaches.
 All three methods are unsatisfactory. We also use the patterns of submission or resistance.

❖ Our non-verbal styles can include the following:
 — accuser
 — drama queen or drama king
 — reasoner
 — victim
 Each style uses a characteristic pattern of gesture and body posture.

❖ Another classic style of verbal language is the use of sensory-based language such as:
 — visual
 — auditory
 — feeler
 — thinker

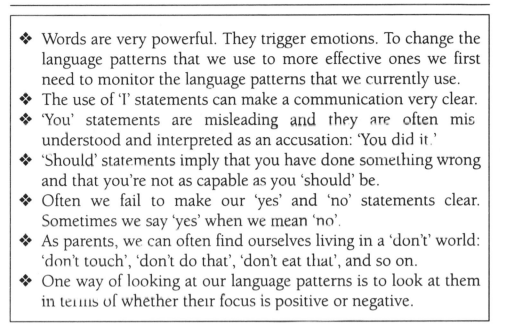

❖ Words are very powerful. They trigger emotions. To change the language patterns that we use to more effective ones we first need to monitor the language patterns that we currently use.

❖ The use of 'I' statements can make a communication very clear.

❖ 'You' statements are misleading and they are often mis understood and interpreted as an accusation: 'You did it.'

❖ 'Should' statements imply that you have done something wrong and that you're not as capable as you 'should' be.

❖ Often we fail to make our 'yes' and 'no' statements clear. Sometimes we say 'yes' when we mean 'no'.

❖ As parents, we can often find ourselves living in a 'don't' world: 'don't touch', 'don't do that', 'don't eat that', and so on.

❖ One way of looking at our language patterns is to look at them in terms of whether their focus is positive or negative.

CHAPTER FIVE

Barriers to Learning and Change

Has there ever been a time in your life when you wanted something quite badly but in order to get it you would have to change in some way? Were you prepared to change to have what you wanted? Surprisingly enough, even though we may want something desperately it seems that the word 'change' evokes so much fear in us that we would prefer the devil we know than the devil we don't know. The thought of having to change brings with it some form of risk. Maybe we will lose something if we change?

For many parents, the desire to change the way in which they communicate with their children often comes out of extreme circumstances of communication breakdown and stress. They realise that the way in which they are currently communicating just isn't working. It isn't getting their kids to cooperate or do what they want and it certainly isn't contributing to a happy and peaceful family life. Unfortunately, the parent is rare who wishes to learn new skills and who openly accepts that to do this they will need to make considerable changes. Due to the history and beliefs that have surrounded parents' attitudes to children, many parents would prefer to continue to blame their children for the breakdown in communication and stress in the family. Fortunately, new awareness and literature on the area of parenting has brought some parents to question the good old days and has encouraged a desire to learn new

86

communication skills as a means of parents accepting personal responsibility for their part in the family's level of communication or miscommunication.

So what does this all mean? It means that in merely reading this book you have shown interest and commitment in developing new communication skills. Pat yourself on the back and celebrate. Even more importantly, you have shown some willingness to face the monster fear of *change*. In order to do this we need to explore exactly what it is that holds us back from change, that is to say, what gets in our way.

While on the Talking with Kids program, parents develop a close bond which allows them to talk openly about their feelings and concerns. Following are some of the feelings of the parents on the course in relation to change. Maybe you will relate some of these comments to your own life:

Judy: I'm scared of changing because I feel like it's going to take up so much of my time. I'm already strung out. I don't need any more hassles. Why can't I just take a pill and it'll all be fixed? I just can't spare the time that I know it's going to take to change. People don't change overnight.

Lloyd: My kids are 10 and 12. If I start changing all of a sudden they're going to think I'm weird. They'll think I've gone crazy if I suddenly start talking to them differently, and then I'll look stupid and I'll be in a worse mess than I am already.

Susan: I'm here because my husband dragged me along. I don't think people change. I don't want to change. As far as I'm concerned, Jack's kids will just have to shape up and start doing what they're told. That's all there is to it. I've told Jack it's either them or me.

Trisha: For me, it's not a question of changing or not. I know that something has to change in our family. We can't go on the same way that we have been going. It's just not working. So I'm prepared to spend the time that it takes. What I am scared of is, what if I can't do it? What if I can't do all of these new skills? What if I fail? I was never very good at school. But at least I'm prepared to try. You guys will have to help me a lot. I'm not a fast learner.

Ted: Yeah. Well, I really want to change. But my business is really booming at the moment and I don't know where I'm going to get the time to change. I thought that I'd change on the course this weekend and that's all the time I'd need to spend. I know I have changed on this weekend, but now I know it's gonna take practice at home as well. I just don't know where I'm going to find the time. While I'm busy working on these new skills I could be losing business and money.

Marilyn: One of the things that I learned yesterday on the course was that I have quite a vested interest in there being drama in my household. Even feeding the family cat can be a main event in my house. The thing is if I change the way I talk and things become more peaceful, I might not be able to cope. Without all the drama I'm scared that I'm going to feel kind of dead inside. Drama's what I'm used to.

Katie: I couldn't be bothered, you know. I thought that I'd come along to this workshop and you'd just fix me or something. I don't want to have to work at it. You should be able to fix me. That's what I came here for.

Steven: I'm worried that if I give my kids more of a free hand then I won't have control any more. They might take over. Then where would I be? Gee, I don't want to feel like they're controlling me. They're my kids, not my boss.

As you can see, the feedback from these parents reveals some of their major beliefs. Let's look at some of these more closely.

Judy has a belief that people don't change easily. She believes that change has to be a struggle and a time-consuming exercise.

Lloyd is worried about looking stupid in front of his kids. He's assumed that his kids won't react favourably to the changes that he is going to make. He's already made the decision for them without even giving them the benefit of the doubt.

Susan is different from the rest of the group in that she didn't really want to be on the course anyway. She was forcing her husband to make a choice between her and his children. A dangerous thing to do. My feeling is that Susan was really scared that Jack might spend more time with his kids and pay them more attention if he were to use all of the skills that he learned on the course. She was scared that she would be left out in the cold and, in actual fact, by forcing Jack to choose she made this inevitable.

Trisha had a belief that said she was a slow and poor learner. As soon as she was in a situation of learning new skills, like being at school, she would be fearful and feel inadequate.

Ted's reason for not changing was time and money. Two very common objections that parents come up with.

Marilyn had a fear of losing her identity. Who was she if she wasn't the ranting, raving, screaming drama queen of a mother? As we shall see later, Marilyn discovered that there was a peaceful and fulfilling life after the drama had been removed from the equation.

Katie had the belief that she was at the workshop to be fixed and that it was up to us to fix her with as little effort on her part as possible. She showed very little motivation in participating in any of the workshop activities, and as a result, made few changes to her behaviour and communication effectiveness.

Steven was scared that his kids might gain control and then where would he be? It seems that he suffered at the hands of an overcontrolling boss and was scared that he might create a similar situation in his home life.

All of these scenarios are typical of the types of fears and objections that parents have to changing the way that they communicate with their children. Can you imagine what your own fears and objections might be? What challenges do you think you would face in your efforts to learn new skills? Are these supported by any of the beliefs that you wrote down about yourself and your attitudes to children in Chapter 1? Beliefs are exactly that, just beliefs, and they can easily be changed once we realise that many of them are not our own. They came instead from role modelling and taking on our parent's beliefs as if they were our own.

Fear of Losing Control

One of the most common barriers to learning and change is the parents' fears of losing the control and power that they have over their children. There is no doubt that parents experience quite a significant amount of power over their children for reasons which I'd like to discuss with you here.

First of all, as a parent you are the one who holds your child's survival in the balance. Your child is fully dependent upon you for all of his or her basic needs. He depends on you for food, shelter, **clothing** and for love and approval. Because of this, your child is **forced** to comply with your wishes so that he can survive in this world.

A sad state of affairs but true. You as parents definitely have the upper hand. Not only are your children dependent on you for material things in order to survive, they are dependent upon you emotionally. Children experience their parents as much bigger than they are and by this I don't just mean physically bigger, although this of course is true. Children experience their parents as psychologically bigger. They tend to see their mothers and fathers as almighty beings who can do no wrong. This forces us as parents to live up to a standard that is unrealistic. We are not gods and we are not perfect.

Many parents spend their time struggling to keep up the appearance of perfection in front of their children because they fear that not only will their children be disillusioned by the truth, but that they the parents will lose their control over the children. Almost entirely up until the time that the child moves into the world as an independent being, his parents have a degree of power and control over him. Parents also wield the power of being able to hurt their more helpless counterparts by withholding basic needs from them or by physically hurting them in some way. By far the most common form of withholding seems to be emotional, and for this reason I consider it to be the most insidious of all.

We all are guilty of bribery and corruption when it comes to getting a child to do something that we want. We all positively reinforce the behaviours that we want to see more of, and negatively reinforce the behaviours that we want to get rid of.

By this I mean that we give a child a lolly when we approve of what he's done and we give him a disapproving look or smack when we disapprove of what he's done. This practice arose from the advice of behavioural scientists who were far more interested in the response of a rat than in the application of their techniques to the welfare of family relations. Lollies and smacks are not the answer.

It's not surprising that parents are fearful about losing control over their children. The fear is that they will turn into rebellious, wild, uncontrollable children who will wreak havoc wherever they go. When there are no limitations or guidelines set by the parent this is usually what happens. These children do become out of control and have difficulty existing effectively in our society. It is clear that a balance needs to be struck between parent and child cooperation. Children do not want limits to be set upon them, rather they would prefer to set their own limits in view of how their behaviour affects their parents. That is to say, there is a big difference between a parent saying, 'Don't you dare interrupt me while I'm talking to another adult. If you do it again you'll get a smack' and the parent saying, 'I don't like it when you interrupt me when I'm talking to my friends. I think it's rude and it makes me angry'.

Many parents justify their use of power by saying that it's in the child's best interests. These parents say that they have a responsibility to society to influence their children with their power. They advocate the 'father knows best' attitude. These parents don't understand that parental power is in fact not influencing their children, but rather it is merely coercing them into prescribed types of behaviour. Power does not convince, educate, nurture or motivate children in any way. When children become adolescents they begin to resist their parents' power and usually become physically too big to be forced into certain behaviours. This is why many teenagers are seen to rebel and why some even break the law to find ways to rebel against their parents' power.

Parents on the Talking with Kids programs admitted that when they used power they often felt guilty and that they felt it was really ineffective in the long run as a means of parenting their children. Then why does the parental control method still exist? I believe it's because most parents have never had an experience themselves of resolving conflict without the use of power, that their own parents always used power over them, and up until now they've not had a workable practical substitute to use in dealing with their family conflicts. This is changing as we move further towards to the year 2000.

So, in summary it's clear to see that one of the greatest barriers to change is that we may have to risk giving up our control over our children. For many parents this is a scary thought.

Parental Apathy

Another barrier to change is apathy. It is true that it is difficult to help someone who isn't willing to help themselves. People such as Katie who come to our workshops with the desire 'to be fixed' soon discover that they are not part of the group. They usually feel this way because they are not prepared to participate and contribute and, of course, they end up getting out of it what they put into it, which may be very little. Some parents sit back and expect their children to change their behaviour to suit them and they are not prepared in the least to alter their own behaviour. These parents rarely find positive changes occurring in their communication skills because they don't put in any effort to make these changes occur.

Premature Closure

Another barrier to change is called 'premature closure'. The parent who does this closes off his mind too early when new information is given to him. He fails to develop any new skills because he thinks that he's got it all sewn up. He knows all that there is to know about parenting just because he's been a parent for 20 years. My only comment here is that we assume people are wise because they are old, but that isn't necessarily so. Well, the same applies to people who have been parenting for a long while. Just because they've been doing it for a long time doesn't mean that they've been doing it effectively.

Self-knowledge

Another factor that limits our ability to learn and to change is the degree of knowledge that we have about ourselves. If we don't know who we really are, what our beliefs and values are, then how can we have a baseline on which to compare the behaviour of others? How can we fully appreciate the beliefs and values of others? How can we judge in any way the behaviour of others when we don't have insights into our own behaviours?

All of the information that I have been asking you to record about yourself has been building up as a useful reference system of information about who you are and what you want. This information is essential if we're to change our communication skills. This information is also great to go back and look at as tangible proof that we have changed our communication skills.

The Fear of Change Itself

As we have seen in earlier pages, change or the very thought of change can be unsettling. This is because changing causes us to step out of our 'comfort zones'. This simply means that we are doing something that is out of the ordinary, and for many of us it feels a little uncomfortable. When we are within our comfort zones we are doing what we've always done and we look, sound and feel comfortable. To challenge you even further to step out of your comfort zone I would like you to delve deeper into yourself and bring to the surface more insights into your own behaviour. But first, a practical demonstration of what the comfort zone can feel like. This is a demonstration commonly used to illustrate what I mean by stepping out of your comfort zone and it works beautifully.

Cross your arms how you would normally cross your arms and just notice how that feels. Now, cross your arms again but this time put the arm that you usually put on top, underneath. How does that feel? Is it comfortable? Most people find the second alternative feels a little strange or a little uncomfortable. However, if they were to do it a number of times they would very quickly get used to it and it would feel comfortable to them. Changing the way in which we communicate can be just like this experience of folding the arms in a new and different way.

Self-knowledge: Exercises and Information

How we communicate with others has a lot to do with how we feel about ourselves, how we get our meaning across and how we treat our feelings. Firstly, let's look at how we feel about ourselves.

- Write down the first 10 adjectives that come into your mind when you think of positive things about yourself. Go ahead and write them now.

- Now write down 10 negative adjectives about yourself.

Sometimes just writing down these lists of words can be very revealing.

- If you were to choose your preferred method for dealing with your own feelings, which would you choose?
  — I say how I feel easily and honestly. I ask for what I want.
  — I squash down my feelings. I think that it's weakness and not right to show anger or tears, especially in front of others. I usually don't ask straight out for what I want.
  — I get angry very easily. I often blame others when I express my anger.

- If you were to choose your preferred method of communication what would it be?
  — I manipulate others to get what I want.
  — I influence others with integrity.
  — I tell others what they 'should' do.
  — I give other people the third degree.
  — I praise other people to get them to do what I want them to do.
  — I persuade others to agree with me by using logic and facts.
  — I avoid confrontations by changing the subject or talking about irrelevant details.
  — I avoid confrontations and decision-making by appearing confused a lot.
  — I refuse to talk about any of my problems with others.

If you agreed that your preferred method of dealing with your feelings was to either squash them down or to blame others, and that your preferred method of communication was to manipulate others with hysteria or with logic, or to praise others to get what you want or to give other people the third degree, then chances are you like being 'in control'. It will give you an idea of where your communication patterns may be breaking down and how much you rely on the use of power to communicate with your children. Chances are also that you will have an objection to learning to communicate without the use of control and power.

If your preferred method of dealing with your feelings was to say how you feel easily and honestly and your preferred method of communication was to influence others with integrity, then chances are you're probably already communicating in a way that resolves family conflicts successfully. You probably don't have a big issue about being in control and you probably are willing to learn new behaviours if you see that they will add value to your life and the lives of the people that you care about.

Below is a list of questions that when answered will provide you with more information about yourself. In particular, these answers will give you information about how your brain processes the information that it receives. The information that you will gain from completing the answers to these questions will give you valuable information about how you think, feel and react in this world.

- The answer to this question will tell you something about what type of job you would tend to enjoy and what sorts of hobbies would be big on your list. It will tell you the areas that you are likely to expect your children to be interested in and give you some ideas as to why they may not want to do the same activities that you want to do. The information in the answer to this question will tell you what your primary interest is, that is the thing that you are most likely to be interested in. For example, do you prefer activity, people, places, things or information. Let's see.

If you were planning a holiday, what would be of most importance to you?
- the place that you were to visit
- the people or person that you would go with
- what you would learn by going there
- what activities that you would do there
- what you would buy there

So, as you can see, there can be a range of different preferences which will affect people's choices in a given situation. Next time you ask what your family members want to do on the weekend, don't be surprised to hear a number of different answers. Your four-year-old may want to play with the child next door, your 12-year-old may want to read a book and your 16-year-old may want to go shopping. Everyone is different, and if we can find out what each person wants then it's quite simple to find some way of meeting everyone's needs.

- The answer to the following question will tell you if the thing that motivates you is a move towards positive rewards or a move away from consequences.

What do you look for in a relationship?

If your answer to this is characterised by the things that you do want and things that are positive, then your motivation is classed as a 'move towards' motivation. This is to say, you are motivated towards the positive things connected with the relationship. If your answer included much of what you don't want to have or it contained many negatives, then your primary motivation is classed as a 'move away' motivation. This is to say that you are motivated by a movement away from certain facets of a relationship. You are moving away from what you don't want to have in a relationship.

This idea of either move towards or move away can be applied to any situation in your life and your response to it may vary depending on the context. For example, in a relationship you may be move-towards motivated, and in work commitments you may be very move-away orientated.

The move towards and move away has a lot to do with your parenting style. You would tend to use these attitudes to motivate your children, that is, you would use rewards or consequences.

- The answer to the following question will give you a clue as to how you prefer to chunk information in your brain, that is, in small chunks or in large chunks.

If you were given a project to do would you be interested in asking your boss about the overall picture of the job — that is, the big picture — or would you be more interested in the specifics of the job requirements?

If you chose the first option, then it's likely that you tend to prefer a global outlook on things. If you chose the second option, then you prefer to know the specifics. The brain chunks information globally or specifically.

Now how does this impact upon your communication with your children? Well, your child may like to be given lots of specific details about what you want him to do and you may only be providing the big picture. Similarly, if he looks bored while you're explaining things in intricate detail it may be that he only needs the big picture to carry out whatever it is you're asking him to do.

- The answer to the next question will tell you something about your relationship to time.

If someone were to arrive for an appointment with you five minutes late would you consider them to be late or not? If you said 'yes' then chances are that you are someone who is very aware of how time passes. Maybe you wear a good-sized watch or you find yourself very organised by the clock. You relate to time as though it were stretched out before you for you to easily monitor. If you felt that the person was not late, then chances are that you are someone who lives more for the moment and maybe you're not so preoccupied with the passing of time. Are your children very aware of how time passes or do they live in the moment? This may have some bearing on how they organise and spend their time. You may need to give the child who lives in the moment plenty of warning before it's time to leave home so that you're not waiting around for him to get organised when it's time for you to leave.

Another extremely useful thing to know about yourself is if you are an introvert or an extrovert. This will govern what sort of job you do, what sorts of hobbies you enjoy, your style of communicating with others and therefore your parenting style.

If you are not comfortable in crowds and would prefer to spend your time alone or with just one other person that you feel comfortable with, then chances are that you're an introvert. If you love parties and spending time with people then you are likely to be an extrovert. Your children will also be introverts or extroverts and this will govern how they react in certain situations in their life. An extroverted child may be very confident about going to birthday parties and an introverted child may find this quite a challenge. An extroverted child may get very bored at home on his own and always want to have friends around and an introverted child may need lots of quiet times alone. Once you know this information about yourself and the other members of your family then you can accommodate communication styles to suit both your own and theirs.

Some of us are very intuitive and we make quick logical leaps in our minds to connect one thought to another. Others of us need to experience something by doing it before we have a full understanding of it. If you like to make plans in your head and you learn very quickly by just listening to information once, then you are probably someone who learns intuitively. If you like to have a more hands-on experience and be shown what to do, then you may be more sensate in how you do things. This is extremely useful information to have in terms of your children's style of learning and how you might be functioning in helping them with their homework. For example, you may understand things very quickly and only need to be told about it once, but your child may need to have a practical demonstration of it before he starts to get a clearer idea of what he's learning.

Some of us make decisions based upon our feelings only and others of us make decisions based upon facts only. The most useful way of making a decision is to have a balance between these two. Which style of decision-making do you think you use? How do your children make their decisions? Is it different from how you make decisions or is it the same? This can be a useful thing to know when helping your children to make their own decisions. Encourage them to have a balance by using the style that they normally don't use and factoring it into the decision-making process.

Key Points

❖ Change brings with it some form of risk.

❖ For some parents, the desire to change the way in which they communicate with their children often comes out of extreme circumstances of communication breakdown and stress.

❖ Common excuses for not wanting to change include:
   — I don't need any more hassles.
   — I don't have the time.
   — People don't change really.
   — I don't want to change.
   — They'll think I've gone crazy.
   — I'll look stupid.
   — What if I can't do all of these new skills?
   — What if I fail?
   — I could lose business and money while I'm busy working on developing these new skills.
   — I couldn't be bothered.
   — I'm worried that the kids might get control and take over.

❖ The fear of losing control of and power over one's children is the most commonly reported reason for the fear of change.

❖ Children see their parents as psychologically bigger, thus forcing their parents to live up to a standard that is unrealistic.

❖ Children would prefer to set their own limits in view of how their behaviour affects their parents.

❖ Parental power doesn't influence children. It coerces them into prescribed forms of behaviour.

❖ Apathy and the attitude 'you fix it for me' does not support any positive change in a parent's communication skills.

❖ Premature closure — that is, the closing off of the mind too early to new information — is a barrier to change.

❖ Information regarding who you are and what you want as a parent or teacher is crucial if you're to change your communication skills.

❖ Change causes us to step out of our 'comfort zone'.

❖ How we communicate with others has a lot to do with how we feel about ourselves and how we deal with our own feelings.

CHAPTER SIX

How to Manage Emotions

Your children are going to try you, test you, pester you and frustrate you at times. There is no question about that. They will probably encourage you at one time or another to experience at least once, all of the large negative emotions of anger, frustration, sadness or fear. The reason why I'm not dealing with positive emotions in this chapter is probably self-evident. We never seem to have difficulties arising from the expression of positive emotions. So what do we do about the negative ones?

Because as adults the feelings that we have and the way that we choose to behave are much more under our own control, our response to our child's behaviour is very much a matter of attitude, thought and choice. Even though frustration and anger are normal reactions, it's not so much the set of events that trigger them but how we choose to deal with them. There are various ways of dealing with these feelings of frustration and anger whenever they come up. Let's explore some of them.

When you feel frustrated and angry at your child, what do you focus on? Do you, like most parents, focus on the child's bad behaviour and how you reacted to it, or do you focus on how you would like her to behave? In many ways, focusing on the bad behaviour, which of course we can't go back and change, is rehearsing the negatives, rehearsing the failures. If we do this enough, we program ourselves to repeat these failures. Redirecting our time and energies into finding positive solutions is a way of being proactive rather than reactive.

One alternative to taking out our frustration and anger on our kids is to plan our response in advance. Most of our emotional responses to our children's poor behaviour is very much reactive. We fly off the handle and we may react instantly with hurtful verbal abuse.

When we plan our response ahead of time we are taking the first steps to being more truly in control of the situation, because we are not merely responding as a knee-jerk reaction but in a thoughtful way. This is called being proactive. It means that we think about our response before we respond.

Of course it's so much easier to change if we actually plan specifically how we want to change and how we are going to change. Identify well in advance how you are going to respond next time your child stirs up your emotions. Are you going to fly off the handle? Are you going to stop and think before you speak? Are you going to take positive action to respond differently from how you would normally respond? Think about this by answering the following questions and then write down some notes about how you would like to respond. Think about the answers in terms of how you would like to look, talk and feel at the end of your reaction to your child's behaviour. Do you want to look frustrated? Do you want to have said a lot of angry words and feel guilty afterwards? Do you want to look relaxed? Do you want to have used positive and constructive talk and feel powerful and positive afterwards? The choice is all yours.

- What would I like to say, do and feel at the next incident of frustration?
- What improvement will I make at the next incident of frustration?

Attitude

Once you are clear on how you want to react and also on how you would like your child's behaviour to have changed, then it is useful to consider attitude. Attitude is everything. It is vital in using this particular approach that you have a hopeful attitude that your changes will work. Otherwise, guess what? They won't work. If I say to myself, 'Well, I don't see any point in working out how I want to change because the children aren't going to change anyway' then I am not willing to change. If I say to myself, 'Well, I'm going to give some of these new things a try and see how my kids react as I think it might just work' then chances are it will work. Remember, the first step in being proactive is to consider your attitude and then plan accordingly.

An important factor to consider in your plan of action is the marked effect of your 'self-talk'. Self-talk is what we say to ourselves inside our heads. Changing our self-talk is a very useful way of changing how we react to a potential 'danger zone' situation. Most of our powerful emotions feed off our self-talk. We all do this self-talk. It doesn't mean we are crazy and hearing voices in our heads, it's a normal part of our brain function and it very much affects our own behaviour.

To make this concept of self-talk clear, let's look at some example scenarios.

Rose was supposed to feed the dog and clean up her room before her father came home from golf. When Joe got home he found that the dog had been fed but that Rose had gone next door to play with her friend Susan without so much as touching her room. Joe immediately went into a lot of self-talk that fuelled his frustration with Rose; for example, 'That kid is so lazy, she *never* does what she's told. She's *always* getting out of doing her chores. Not this time. I'm going to stop her watching TV or riding her bike for a week. That will teach her to be such a rebel.'

Worse still, Joe ranted and raved like this when his wife got home from day shift so not only did he become frustrated, but he whipped his wife into a frenzy as well. She said, 'I don't know why I have to put up with this. I should have stayed at work. These kids are selfish and inconsiderate. They never appreciate what I do. I spend all day Saturday at work trying to earn money to take these kids on a holiday and this is the thanks I get.'

Now you may agree that Joe and his wife had every reason to be angry at Rose, but if we look at their self-talk what we find is a lot of labelling. For example, Rose was labelled lazy and a rebel, and then both children were labelled selfish and inconsiderate. What this labelling does is to reinforce Joe's and his wife's negative view of their children and makes them even more frustrated.

Such is the power of language. What's more, when we label our children we then start looking for more behaviours that support that label and the cycle goes on and on. Another factor of Joe and his wife's self-talk is the 'exaggeration factor'. Whenever we use the words 'always' or 'never', the exaggeration factor is probably coming into play. It is very unlikely that Rose *never* does what she's told or

106

that she *always* gets out of doing her chores. It's also unlikely that both the children *never* appreciate what their mother does for them. Magnifying your child's misbehaviour only serves to increase your level of frustration. It's more useful for all concerned if you try to keep your self-talk based upon hard facts and not assumptions or exaggerations.

Using a trigger word in our self-talk can help us delay those knee-jerk reactions. If when we become frustrated we say to ourselves 'stop and think' then chances are we are more likely to react in different ways from the past. A highly useful example of self-talk to employ is to ask yourself after you have utilised some of your new ways of dealing with your child's behaviour whether your response this time improved from the previous frustration experience. When we answer this question with self-talk, then we are more likely to turn off the negative self-talk and take the time to employ alternative methods such as the next one, which is called 'focusing'.

The Focusing Technique

The focusing technique is one which requires very little skill to use. It's quick and easy and all you require is a quiet spot where you can sit and be on your own to think. Because it usually only takes about one minute to perform, it's a good alternative to choose to use when the children, partner or boss bring up unwelcome emotions in you, such as anger, frustration or sadness. The beauty of this technique is that you can teach your children to use it on themselves from about seven years of age onwards or you can guide them through it. A mature five- or six-year-old might be able to be guided through it, but it depends very much upon the individual child.

Begin by finding a comfortable chair to sit in, in as quiet a place as possible. You then go inside yourself and ask 'What am I feeling?' When you get a sense of what the feeling is about, put a name to it; for example, frustration. Once you have done that, establish where in your body you are feeling that emotion; for example, the stomach. When you have labelled the emotion and found its location, then move on to ask yourself 'What's under that?' That is, what's under the first feeling. Again, establish where in the body you are feeling this emotion.

Continue to do this until you get to what seems like the bottom-line emotion. For example, someone may start off by feeling the emotion of frustration and then hey discover that under that is anger and then under that is sadness. The location of the emotion may move; for example, from the stomach to the solar plexus and then up to the heart. Finding the bottom-line emotion for you may only take a matter of seconds and for someone else it may take anything up to 20 minutes.

Once you have established the bottom-line emotion, the best possible thing you can do is to sit with it. Some people find that they need to express the emotion in some way and maybe that means shouting or crying, whatever is appropriate. There will, of course, be situations where you can't appropriately express the emotion at that time. You will need to wait until you get home to actually sit down and find out exactly what's going on. Many times when parents find themselves in the situation of getting angry at their children, if they could take two minutes to sit down and focus before they lashed out at their children they may discover that the anger really had nothing at all to do with the children but was about something their partner or their workmate said earlier in the day. Focusing is a much better alternative to the old 'count to 10' idea as that method doesn't encourage you to push down your emotion or to negate it. It merely gets you to take a pause and really look at what's going on for you.

Even in today's society it is still not acceptable to express our emotions openly. As well as the poisonous pedagogy, we have inherited from our parents the belief that we can and cannot safely express some emotions and, of course, we pass this on to our own children. Now that there is more and more evidence to link diseases such as heart disease and cancer to the storage in the body of negative emotions, there is even more reason to allow ourselves and our children to fully express their emotions.

There are many ways to teach a child how she can release negative emotions without damaging herself or others. When a child is angry, instead of letting her punch up on her little brother or instead of smacking her yourself and thereby setting up a perfect example of aggression for her to follow, you can take her into the bedroom and get her to beat up her pillow. This way the child releases the emotion from her body. The emotion is not internalised and squashed down, nor is it negated. It is understandable that your eight-year-old would be angry if her two-year-old brother had destroyed one of her best games. Instead of picking on her little brother, she can more appropriately express her anger by beating up her pillow and shouting at her brother into the pillow if she needs to. This may sound crazy to parents who are used to smacking their children or to parents who don't allow the expression of negative emotions in their household, but it's simple, it works and it is more physically and emotionally healthy than any other technique that I know of.

Similarly, it is necessary to allow a child to experience sadness. What we tend to do, of course, is take on our child's problem as our own and when they feel sad then we feel sad. It's very distressing to see anyone that you care about in pain. So many times we try to stop our children from crying, but it is more than likely that one of the reasons we want them to stop feeling so bad is because it will make us feel better if they feel better. However, when we cry certain chemicals are released in our tears that have a calming and restorative effect upon the human body and so yet again there is evidence to support that it is far more healthy to express the emotion than suppress the emotion.

Below is an example of a man and his wife using the technique of focusing. Michael is guided through it by his wife Julie:

Julie: What's going on, Michael?

Michael: I feel angry.

Julie: Where in your body do you feel the anger?

Michael: It's in my arms and my stomach.

Julie: What's under the anger, Michael?

Michael: Umm, I'm not sure. It's sort of loneliness.

Julie: Where in your body is the loneliness situated, Michael?

Michael: It's near my heart.

Julie: What's under the loneliness, Michael?

Michael: It's fear. Yes, it's definitely fear. I'm scared of losing you because we've been arguing so much lately.

Julie: Where do you feel the fear, Michael?

Michael: It's in my stomach.

Now there is quite a difference between the anger that Michael first felt and the bottom-line emotion of fear. As a result of this procedure, which took all of three minutes, Julie and Michael were then able to discuss why they had been arguing so much lately and what was really at the bottom of that. When Michael performed the focusing technique on Julie, they both discovered that she too had been worried about their recent bout of arguments and that she was not only scared but very sad and guilty about them.

Here is an example of a father taking his seven-year-old son through the process:

Dad: Okay John, just sit back and close your eyes. Now, how do you feel right now?

John: I feel confused.

Dad: Where is the confusion in your body? It might be in your stomach or your arms or legs or anywhere in your body.

John: It's in my head, Dad.

Dad: Okay, good boy, you're doing really well. What's under the confusion, John?

John: I don't know. It's changing. It's changing to being angry.

Dad: So where do you feel the anger?

John: It's in my stomach.
Dad: What's under the anger, John?
John: I feel angry 'cause I got in trouble and it wasn't my fault. Now I just feel sad. Nobody believed me.
Dad: Where do you feel the sadness?
John: It's here (*pointing to heart area*)
John starts to cry and Dad just holds him.
Dad: Good boy, let it all out. It's okay to be sad.

This is a good example of a father allowing his son to cry without instilling in him the old stereotype of 'boys don't cry'. This will allow John to release the emotion and to feel much better. It also confirms to John that his assessment of the situation is correct. He knows that he's sad and that's okay. Nobody is telling him that he's not sad or that it's not okay to be sad.

It takes a lot of courage to use the focusing technique on both yourself and your children if there has been a tendency in your household to ignore, disguise or suppress emotions in any way. In the long term, this is a far wiser choice than repressing the unwanted emotion. Most parents find that they can begin to change the way in which they deal with their children's emotions if they start off slowly and work their way up to changing their style of dealing with emotions. The true test comes when the children start to display their anger or sadness when grandparents or next-door neighbours are around. This is mostly because the parents may feel that they're on show and that their new skills are being judged. If your own parents told you to suppress your emotions then chances are they will not approve of your modern methods of handling your child.

The choice is yours. You can revert back to old behaviours or you can sit the grandparents down and explain to them that you've looked into this carefully and that this is the way you want to deal with your children's emotions from here on in. Would they please support you and try to deal with the children in a similar manner. Teach your own parents about the beating-the-pillow idea. They may want to use it themselves when their spouse gets on their nerves. It sure beats shouting at one another.

Emotions in Children

Children experience the very same emotions that we do but they often express them differently. It is important that parents teach children the value of their emotions. Tell them that anger is important. Anger makes us stand up for ourselves and protect ourselves. Fear is also very important in the correct context. It helps us get out of the way of a speeding truck. It keeps us from taking severe risks that may damage us. Sadness is also important because the expression of sadness allows us to clear ourselves. It literally washes us clean when we have an unhappy experience occur. It allows us to express an emotion and then get up and get on with our lives, reforming contact with other individuals.

When the emotions of anger, fear and sadness are expressed appropriately, it makes room for the expression of those positive emotions that I mentioned, especially that of joy. Many parents find that they may be able to use alternative strategies for dealing with their own negative emotions, but apart from taking their child through the technique of focusing they are lost for ways to help their children deal with their emotions. As a result of this, the children miss out on feeling good about themselves. To understand how we can help our children feel good about themselves and to deal with their own negative emotions, we need to firstly understand where their feelings come from. Let's look more closely at this.

It seems that our emotional responses come very much from our beliefs. These beliefs are built up very much from a child's past experiences. For example, if Billy goes to stay over at a friend's house and he becomes distraught and has an asthma attack, then he may link the event of staying over at a friend's house to having an asthma attack. Next time he's invited to stay over at a friend's house, he may feel uncomfortable because he will be worried that he may have another asthma attack. Of course each child responds differently to the very same situation based upon their past experiences and the beliefs that result from these. For example, if Julie and Vicky are invited to a picnic, Julie may see the picnic as a fun opportunity to meet new friends and eat yummy food. Vicky, on the other hand, may see the picnic as a situation where she may be left out of games, be eating food that she's not used to and it may be an opportunity to be embarrassed if nobody plays with her at the picnic. Whereas Julie's reaction is one of happy excitement, Vicky's reaction is one of fear and worry. Both children can be in exactly the same situation and, as a result of their beliefs, have very different emotional responses.

Even though we as parents can't protect our children from experiencing situations where they may feel uncomfortable or they may feel worried and fearful, we can influence their beliefs about themselves. If Vicky had a belief about herself that it was safe for her to try new foods and that she was a popular child who usually was asked to join in games, then her response to the picnic invitation may have been very different. Let's look more closely at the part that parents, teachers and society play in setting up a child's belief system.

Children compare their actual achievements with what they think they are capable of achieving. They need to be encouraged to try new things that may be challenging for them. When they discover they can do something that they may have considered challenging, they form a new belief about themselves based upon that result. Children learn to think in either a positive or a negative way based upon the events that happen in their lives and based upon their greatest role model: you, their parents. If a child learns to constantly think that any time she doesn't achieve something with 100 per cent accuracy that this is bad and that consequently she has failed, then she is going to respond to all her achievements, no matter how wonderful they are, in a negative way. Once she gets used to thinking negatively, this way of thinking will become her natural way of thinking and a habit that stays with her for life.

Children start to develop a sense of right and wrong fairly early in life. By praising certain behaviours and ignoring or criticising others, parents and teachers begin to influence the behaviour and the beliefs and values of children. Society plays a strong part in influencing a child to live by the values that it sets. Sometimes these values are not those of the child and they may not meet her true needs, thus resulting in unhappiness and disillusionment. Children often attribute some result to a particular event, like Billy who had the asthma attack while staying at his friend's place. Based on these results, they often make overgeneralisations. They may also negate information from the overall picture or distort the information available. For example, if a child runs a race and she comes third in the race, she may either form a belief that she is a good runner because she came third or overgeneralise and say that she's a poor runner because she failed to come first. She may also delete information by forgetting that she was running against children that were much older and bigger than she is. Effective ways of dealing with this are to encourage your child to express her emotions appropriately and at the same time to build up her self-esteem.

Let's look firstly at the expression of the negative emotions. As anger is often at the forefront, let's deal firstly with that. Kids can be made to feel comfortable with their anger if you follow a few basic handy hints:

- Let them know that hitting is not an acceptable way of them dealing with their anger. No matter how young they are, they need to express their anger in words rather than actions. What isn't expressed with the lips is often expressed with the fists.
- Help them to identity how they feel by using the focusing technique, and help them to identify what went wrong to make them feel that way.
- Always show them by your own example that it's okay to get angry as long as it's done in a useful way. That is to say, Mum and Dad don't hit each other. They discuss and identify how

they feel and the source of these feelings. In other words, Mum and Dad always make an attempt to be the solutions rather than the problem. Your child will learn a more valuable lesson by seeing you express clear anger than they will if you were to never argue in front of them and were always trying to be self-contained and hide your feelings.

- Help them to focus on what they want to have happen instead of what they don't want. When anger isn't directly expressed, it can turn very quickly into manipulation and/or whingeing. Ask them directly what they want and encourage them to be clear about it.

Helping your children to deal with sadness is done by supporting them to express their sadness without telling them to 'grow up', 'be a big man', 'don't be a sook'. Be there for them. Allow them to cry. Hold them if they need you to and leave them alone if they need you to. Ask them what they want.

Our children need to see the world we live in as essentially a safe place. They need to know that it's safe to speak up and get their needs met. At the same time we need to teach them that fear is useful. That they need to look when they cross the road and that they need to be aware of strangers.

Children who feel good about themselves usually have a positive outlook and positive beliefs about their abilities and who they are. They are usually confident and fun to be around. We need to help our children to work out if their fear is justified or if it's an irrational fear. Some handy hints for dealing with fear are as follows:

- Talk plainly about fear and demystify it. Admit that fears exist and that Mum and Dad have fears, too. After all, everyone is scared at some time, even parents.
- If a child raises a fear then talk it over with her. This gives her feedback that her experience is valid in your eyes. That is to say, you are not putting her down for her feelings. You acknowledge that she is fearful if she says she is. From this

point you can work out if the fear is founded on reality or if it's an irrational fear. If it's a real fear then help the child to find some solutions. What does she need to do to feel safe again? If it's an irrational fear then tell her that it's irrational. Don't go looking in cupboards for boogiemen that don't exist, but be honest and clear with her.

Helping Children to Feel Good about Themselves

Now that we've looked at the first part of our challenge, that is how to help our children deal with their emotions, let's tackle the second part. So how do we as parents and teachers help children to feel good about themselves? Essentially, the most effective way of doing this is in how we talk to a child.

One way is to set an example for our children by trying to avoid overgeneralising, deleting and distorting information ourselves. Clear communication results from an effort to be realistic and sticking to the facts.

Using nurturing messages is another very important way to boost self-esteem. This allows the child to see her own increased value in her own eyes and encourages growth and maturity. We need to continually remind ourselves of the importance of the language that we use with our children. Nurturing messages include those messages that are positive. We can give nurturing messages by acknowledging a child's efforts and improvements rather than always looking to the result. Here are some scenarios that highlight the use of acknowledging the child's efforts rather than the result:

John: Here's my report, Mum. What do you think of it?
Mum: Gee, you've really improved in maths and spelling, haven't you? Last time you got a C for both, didn't you? This time you got two B's. That's fantastic. I'm proud of you, John. You've been trying so hard and it's paid off. Good job.

116

John: Thanks, Mum. I'm gonna keep trying hard. It's getting a bit easier, you know.

Dad: How did you go at ballet today, sweetheart?
Caitlin: Okay, Daddy. I didn't do as well as last week. Jodie got a sticker and I didn't.
Dad: Oh, that's a shame. Do you think you tried just as hard as last week?
Caitlin: Yes, I think I did, Daddy.
Dad: Well darling, if you tried your best and you enjoyed the class, then that's a whole lot more important to me than any sticker.
Caitlin: You know, Daddy. I think you're right. I had a good time and I really worked hard.

A second way to help your child feel good about herself is to focus on the positive strengths that she has rather than focus on her weaknesses. A good rule of thumb is to always give positive feedback first, and then if you need, give constructive criticism second. It's always best to give the positive feedback straightaway, as soon as your child has done something helpful or kind. Keep an eye out for the little things that your child does. Every little bit of praise adds up.

A third and very useful thing to do with your children is to give them set responsibilities around the home and include them in the 'team' that is your family. Even really little children can be given quite small tasks to do of which they can then feel proud of as their contribution to the family. Doing this will help you to avoid burnout as well, as the household chores are more equally distributed instead of all falling onto Mum's or Dad's shoulders. Of course, once the task is completed it will provide you with an opportunity to offer praise and comments on how the children are improving in doing their jobs.

Another essential ingredient in helping your child feel good about herself is to involve her in problem-solving. Accept all comments without rejecting any, thus allowing your child to feel good by seeing that you have faith in her abilities. You can show even more faith by encouraging her to do things that would normally be a little challenging for her. Let her know that you have enough confidence in her and that she can do this new activity.

One of the most useful ways to build a child's self-esteem is to both encourage and accept any new ideas that she has. No matter how outrageous they might seem to you, your child's ideas are very valid to her. Some parents are easily shocked by their child's ideas and react suddenly with a negative response:

Caitlin: Mummy I'm going to be an actress when I grow up.
Mum: Of course you're not going to be an actress. Don't be silly.

By not expressing outright disapproval of your child's ideas, you are acknowledging her individuality and her right to have an opinion. Remember also that she's a child trying to make some sense of a very adult world. If you show respect for your child's ideas when she's young, then chances are when she becomes a teenager she will respect your ideas.

Earlier on I mentioned how important it was for you as parents and teachers to take a positive attitude to life and to the new communication skills that you are learning. It's vitally important that from very early on we challenge our children's negative beliefs and irrational beliefs so that this negative thinking does not become an entrenched habit. So how do we do this? Remember when we talked about deleting, distorting and overgeneralising information? We can challenge our children's deletions, distortions and generalisations and, in doing so, help them replace their negative beliefs with positive ones.

For example, Judy has an 11-year-old daughter, Margie. Judy noticed that Margie was spending a lot of time moping around the house and lying on her bed looking sad and worried. Being the perceptive mother that she is, Judy concluded that something must be worrying Margie a great deal so she went into Margie's room to have a chat. Margie said that her girlfriend Gill had been ganging up on her and teasing her at school and that this made Margie feel like everyone hated her. This is, of course, an overgeneralisation. Margie also thought that her Mum had been focusing a lot of attention on her work and not on Margie. Margie thought that Judy didn't want to spend time with her and that she must find her boring to be around. This too is an overgeneralisation and also a deletion of the vital fact that this month was usually the busiest month of the year at Judy's work and she'd had to spend a lot of extra hours at work. Once Margie was allowed to freely express herself and have a cry, she admitted all of this to Judy. Judy could then go ahead and help Margie see that just because Gill was being mean to her didn't mean that she couldn't ask someone else to play with her and that in fact not *everyone* hated her at all. Judy could also explain to Margie that she had been extra busy at work and that she would be able to make an effort this week to spend more time with her because she enjoyed spending time with her. All of this was sorted out in a matter of 15 minutes and Margie no longer moped around the house.

Brad was normally a very good student, but his teachers had noticed a marked reduction in his enthusiasm for school. Mrs Major, his class teacher, decided to have a word with him. After some discussion, it was clear that Brad was having difficulty in understanding what was being said in class, not because he was dumb, which was what he had concluded, but because he couldn't hear what Mrs Major was saying and he therefore missed vital information. Mrs Major organised a hearing test for Brad with permission from his mother and father, and the result showed that his seating position in class needed to be changed. Once Brad moved up the front of the class he was fine and his enthusiasm returned. His belief that he was dumb was overruled by the reality that he was a little hard of hearing.

Faith had been complaining of aches and pains for a week. Her father became concerned after she continued to complain well into the following week. The doctor had ruled out any problems and so Faith's father considered that it may be related to something that she was worrying about. Once Faith's father sat down and asked her if anything was worrying her, it all poured out. It seemed that Faith was worrying about the school athletics tryouts that were coming up. She really wanted to make the athletics team, but some of the other kids had told her she wasn't good enough. Faith had the belief that the other kids must be right that she wasn't good enough. She had manufactured the aches and pains so that she could miss the tryouts for the athletics team and not appear a failure. If she didn't make the team it would mean that those other kids were right. Faith's father was able to show her that she needed to believe in herself and her abilities, and to prove to those other kids that she really was good at athletics. Faith changed her belief around to a more positive one and she made the team.

Ben was usually a pretty good eater, but lately his mother had noticed that he barely touched his food and just played with it instead. Once faced with a discussion about this with both his mother and father, Ben revealed that his girlfriend had dumped him and that he was feeling really down about it. Ben's father shared with him a common experience that he had had as a teenager, highlighting the belief he had thought no one would like him if this particular girl didn't. Ben's father showed him that once he changed his belief about not being liked by other girls just because one girl dumped him, he found that there were lots of girls who liked him and wanted to spend time with him. Ben could see that his negative attitude and low feelings would probably make him not all that much fun to be around and that there really were lots of girls who liked him. Once he realised this he shifted his attitude and before long was back to his old self and madly in love with a new girl.

Jackie was a plodder at school. She always worked hard and did her best, but sometimes she would simply give up and succumb to feelings of hopelessness. Every time she started doing this and started commenting on how stupid she was and how her spelling was hopeless, she was never able to do it. Her mother stepped in to change her belief system. She reminded Jackie of how good she was at art and maths, and how last term she had improved her spelling grade from a D to a C. These facts busted Jackie's belief that she was hopeless because they provided undeniable proof that she was not hopeless. Jackie replaced her negative belief about her spelling with a more positive one which said that she had improved and that she would continue working to improve even further.

By using the skills of active listening outlined in Chapter 7, 'A Change for the Better', and the technique of focusing discussed here, you can help your child effectively deal with the negative unwanted emotions by both fully expressing them and then making changes to the context or environment surrounding the situation that is troubling them and to the beliefs surrounding that situation.

How To Help Your Child Deal with Stress

In little doses, stress can be a very positive thing. Sometimes we perform better under stress. When stress builds up and becomes a continual pattern, however, it can lead to negative beliefs, negative thoughts and even poor health. In the long term, stress certainly leads to difficulties with succeeding in the area of your choice. Children experience stress from many different areas, but what parents really want to know is how they can help reduce the stress their children experience on a day-to-day basis. There are some common situations that can induce stress in a child. By being aware of these as parents and teachers, we can prevent the stress from getting out of hand.

Some of the more common stressful situations for children include:

- the birth of a new baby in the family
- the separation and/or divorce of the parents
- someone in the family becomes seriously ill
- being teased at school

- having to go to hospital for any reason
- having difficulties with learning at school
- starting a new term at school or even starting at a new school
- losing your best friend at school or in the neighbourhood
- a family pet having an accident or running away
- a grandparent dying
- moving to a new house and a new neighbourhood
- fighting between parents or brothers and sisters
- a change of teacher midway through the year
- trying out for the school band, choir, drama production or sporting team.

If you notice that your child is having difficulty sleeping, she seems to lack motivation and energy or she seems to constantly worry about future events, then chances are that she may be experiencing the beast called stress. A good way of helping your child monitor when she is stressed is to ask her each night to rate her stress level on a ruler. Use a rating of 1, which is very low, to 10, which is the highest stress level. There are some very simple and effective methods of helping your child to alleviate stress.

One method is to change those negative beliefs around. Another very useful method is to release stress from the body by doing some physical activity a few times a week. This can be any physical activity that the child enjoys, and if she's not physically inclined it can be simple slow walking or even dance classes aimed at exercising but having fun at the same time. The third way of helping your child deal with stress is to teach her to meditate in a very simple and easy way. The child merely sits in a chair or lies in bed and listens to your voice while she relaxes. You take her through a guided visualisation that assists in allowing her to deal with her worries. Do this at least once a night or day for about two weeks, and I recommend that it become a regular part of a child's routine. In this way, you not only alleviate stress when it comes up, but you avoid the build up of stress as you go.

I have included here two of my own guided visualisations that I use with children. They may seem a little young for your 10- or 11-year-old, but you'd be surprised how much children of even this age like to return to the fantasy of younger years. Children as young as three years old have enjoyed these little stories either as a bedtime story, afternoon nap or regular daytime activity.

After you have read your child a visualisation, you can safely leave her to rest for 20 minutes or so, or even longer if she seems to be at peace and the situation is appropriate. If she doesn't wake after half an hour, then you can gently whisper to her that it's time to come back into the room.

The Beautiful Angel Sings to the Moon

As you relax and breathe, listen to my voice and let it paint pictures in your head. These pictures can be coloured or black and white. There is no right or wrong. Whatever picture you make up is absolutely the best picture for you. Now listen to my voice as I tell you this little story. Breathe and relax. Just breathe and relax.

Imagine a beautiful angel, the most beautiful angel in the whole world and universe. She is your guardian angel and she has come to take you on a magical journey. She is holding out her hand to you now. Take her hand and fly up with her. Fly high above the soft white clouds and into the peaceful night, way up towards the moon. She is holding your hand. You are perfectly safe. This is your guardian angel. She will always be there to protect you and look after you.

Right now she is taking you on a wonderful adventure. Zoom past the golden moon and through hundreds and thousands of bright twinkling silver stars. See if you can put out your other hand and touch the stars as you fly past. What do they feel like? Do they shimmer and glimmer between your fingertips? Do they sing as you whiz past them? What does it feel like to be so far above the Earth? So far away from any troubles, any worries, any concerns? Remember to breathe and relax. Just breathe and relax.

Now your guardian angel is about to alight on one of those soft, puffy clouds way, way up where the moon shines brightly and the stars glimmer and twinkle. Ever so gently she helps you to land upon the white, foamy cloud. What does it feel like to be sitting or lying on your very own personal cloud? This is your very own cloud where you can sit or lie, dream beautiful dreams and think wonderful thoughts.

As you relax even further on your cloud, your guardian angel is going to help you throw away any thing that's worrying you to make sure that you have a magical, fun time. So, if you have any little worry or even a big worry, slowly pick it up and toss it over the side of your cloud. Allow it to fall into the night and disappear into the never-ending space of the universe. Take the next worry, no matter how big or small, and toss it over the edge of your cloud and off into the universe. Watch it float away into the distance of the dark night until you can't see it any more. That's right. Now just breathe and relax. Breathe and relax. Now toss away any final worries and concerns, and then, floating gently on your cloud, reach out to the stars. As you do that, hear them sing especially for you, like the voices of a thousand tiny angels they are singing and glittering as they sing.

Your guardian angel is touching your hand gently now because it's time for her to fly home and as she waves goodbye she tells you the secret of how you can float very gently back home whenever you need to. As she leaves she gives you a special gift, one that is very important to you. It has a message attached to it. Open the message gently and read what it has to say. Now as you rest and lie back on your beautiful fluffy cloud think beautiful thoughts and remember your message as you float off to sleep for a short time. When it's time to return home I know that you will breathe and relax, and, bringing your gift with you, very gently just float back down to home and in your own time open your eyes and return to the room. But for now, rest easy and dream beautiful dreams.

Magic Mountain

Just sit back and breathe and relax. We are about to go on a very important journey. One full of adventure and fun. As you relax and breathe I want you to see that in the distance and coming towards you is a little boat. This is your special boat. One that takes you safely on adventures and brings you safely back home again.

Step carefully into the little boat. Make sure that you sit in the most comfortable position on the boat, lie back against the beautiful plush pillows and let the boat steer its own course down the trickling stream. Allow yourself to float with the little boat. Float gently down the stream and listen to the noise of the water as it babbles past the little boat and the stones beneath. Reach your hand over the edge of the boat and feel the water as it flows past your fingertips. What temperature is the water in the little stream?

Now as you float along the stream you notice that at the edge of the stream are some people waving at you. They look at you with love and beckon you to come and join them for some fun and a magnificent picnic of all of your favourite foods and drink. You stay and play with these kind people and you eat as much as you want and drink as much as you want. You have such a fun time playing and romping in the meadow by the stream. These people are actually magical beings and if you tell them your worries they promise to take all of them away with such ease that you wonder where those worries ever came from. Let them take away your worries now. When they have taken your worries from you they give you a very special gift in return. Something wonderful to replace those worries with. I wonder what your special gift might be? Open it now. Isn't it beautiful? It's just for you. Especially for you.

Now take the hands of your special friends and climb up the magic mountain and inside the top of the mountain. Here you will come to a beautiful crystal cave with a glistening stream. It glistens in the sunlight and the rays shine upon you. Feel the rays of sunlight on your face. Now look around and see what you can find to play with in this magical cave. What do you see there? Go over now and play with it for as long as you want to. When you're ready to go home, just let your special friends know and they will walk you back down the mountain and put you safely in your little boat. Remember to bring your gift with you and return home whenever you're ready. I'll leave you now to play in the mountain and discover whatever it is that you discover.

Key Points

❖ Your children will probably encourage you at one time or another to experience, at least once, all of the large negative emotions of anger, frustration, sadness and fear.

❖ As adults our response to our child's behaviour is very much a matter of attitude, thought and choice.

❖ Focusing on the bad behaviour which we can't go back and change is rehearsing the negatives and the failures.

❖ We can be proactive rather than reactive by directing our time and energies into finding positive solutions.

❖ Most of our emotional responses to our children's poor behaviour is very much reactive.

❖ One way to deal with negative emotions is to plan in advance your response. Identify well in advance how you will respond to that particular behaviour when the next situation arises.

❖ Attitude is very important. It is vital in making changes in your reactive behaviour that you have a hopeful attitude that your changes will work.

❖ An important factor to consider in your plans for change is the marked effect of your self-talk.

❖ Changing your self-talk is a very useful way of changing how we react to a potential 'danger zone' situation.

❖ Avoid labelling your children or exaggerating the truth about their behaviour when they do something wrong.

❖ Use a trigger word or phrase such as 'stop and think' to delay your knee-jerk reaction to poor behaviour.

❖ The focusing technique is a quick and easy way to react differently to your child's behaviour and how it makes you feel.

❖ You can teach your children to use the focusing technique on themselves if they're seven years of age or older. You can guide your younger children through the steps yourself.

❖ Focusing requires sitting in a quiet location, labelling your feeling, finding where that feeling is located in the body, finding what's under that feeling and so on until you find the bottom-line emotion. This emotion can then be expressed in some way.

❖ It is undesirable to squash down or negate our expression of feelings.

❖ Our emotional responses come from our beliefs, which are based on our past experiences.

❖ Parents and teachers influence the behaviour, beliefs and values of children by praising certain behaviours and ignoring or criticising others.

❖ Society influences a child to live by its set of values.

❖ All of us overgeneralise, distort and delete information in our minds.

❖ Using nurturing messages is an important way to boost self-esteem.

❖ Acknowledge your child's efforts rather than the results.

❖ Focus on your child's positive strengths rather than on her weaknesses.

❖ Give your child responsibility and include her on the 'team' that is your family.

❖ Involve your child in family problem-solving.

❖ Encourage and accept your child's new ideas.

❖ Challenge your child's deletions, distortions and over-generalising of information, and in so doing, help her replace negative beliefs with positive ones.

❖ If your child is having difficulty sleeping, is lacking in motivation and energy and seems to be constantly concerned, she may be experiencing stress.

❖ Stress can be alleviated by changing negative beliefs, doing regular physical exercise and meditating regularly.

CHAPTER SEVEN

A Change for the Better: Six Steps to a Successful Win–Win Communication

How many times have you felt like you just weren't getting through to your child and that you just weren't on the same wavelength? You ask him to help you with something and sometimes he simply ignores you. You ask him about his day at school and he seems to have nothing to say. You try to get close to him, but he seems on guard, defensive and not interested. Don't worry, you're not alone. In fact, whenever I ask the question, 'How many times have you felt like you just weren't getting through to your children and that you just aren't on the same wavelength?' on a Talking with Kids workshop, almost every person in the room raises a hand. Some parents raise both hands.

Many of us feel that our children just don't listen to us and that they have this strange disease called 'selective listening'. It's true. They do. Ask your 10-year-old to clean up his room and often you're met with a groan, a disapproving look or stony silence. Ask him what sort of ice-cream he wants you to buy for him and you are met with a very different type of attention. Similarly, ask your three-year-old to pack away his Lego and wait for the response. You could be waiting a long, long time. Now try unwrapping a lolly at 50 paces and see if you don't get run over in the stampede.

Children are far more interested in something that they can really relate to or have fun with than they are in being told to clean up their room or turn off the television set. We can't really blame them. Look at their values! Try asking an eight-year-old what's most important to him in life, and you'll probably end up with a list that goes something like this: fun, friends, food, videos, rollerblades, transformers.

And it's true that we, as adults, are very much the same. We are usually more interested in topics that are related to ourselves and our values. As human beings we are almost always interested in 'what's in it for us?'. Children are the same, and if you want to get your child to listen to you then you need to provide the 'what's in it for me?' for him. We need to appeal to our children's values.

There are six major steps in a win–win communication and appealing to your child's values is just one of them. The other steps are knowing your outcome, building rapport, actively listening, being congruent, and using the win–win technique. To know your outcome means simply knowing the result that you want to produce. This can be as simple as 'I want Peter to really listen to what I have to say' or 'I want Caitlin to pick up her toys'.

The next step is to build rapport and this means reducing the differences between yourself and your child. We will be looking more closely at this shortly. The next step is to actively listen, which, as you will see, is very different from selective listening. The next step is to be congruent. Congruency occurs when what we look like, sound like and feel like all match up. The final step is the win–win negotiation procedure, and this is linked closely to our first step of appealing to our child's values. If we combine these steps then we can easily achieve a win–win outcome for all parties concerned, so that all individuals are treated with respect, and an outcome that pleases everyone is achieved with ease.

Values and How To Benefit from Them

Remember in Chapter 1 where you listed your values in relationship to both life in general and then, more specifically, your values relating to children? Well, now I'm going to ask you to use the in-depth knowledge that you have of your own children or the children that you care for to go ahead and hazard a guess at what you think their values might be. Make a list of these values.

Next time you want your child to do something, remember to appeal to his values. For example, next time you want your child to turn off the television, try appealing to his highest value. Many of you may

see this as old-fashioned bribery or brainwashing. It's true that appealing to someone's values is giving them something they want, and if you want to call that bribery, that's fine by me. It is, however, very sophisticated bribery when you appeal to someone's values, because it is much more of a win–win situation. Say for example that your child's highest value is chocolate. When you ask him to turn off that television, appeal to his value by saying something like this: 'I know how much you love chocolate and I thought that if you turn off the television as soon as I ask you to then I would put some chocolate in your lunch box tomorrow. What do you think?'

Now that's a fair exchange, don't you think? If you don't want to give your child chocolate then consider his second most important value: fun. Get really specific about what he considers to be fun. It may be having a friend over to visit, in which case you might say the following: 'I know how much you like having fun and I thought that if you turned the television off as soon as I asked you each night this week, that you might like to have Robby over to stay on Friday night. What do you think?'

Many of you probably already use this technique of appealing to a child's values without even knowing it. It is highly effective if you are accurate in knowing your child's value list and how he ranks his values according to importance. For example, if going to the movies is at the bottom of his value list, don't use it as your first option. If fun is top of his list, then use it at every opportunity and be specific about what he considers fun to be.

Know Your Outcome

To understand just what I mean by knowing your outcome, let's look at a few examples from our case study scenarios.

Martha had an outcome that was to get her three-year-old son just to listen to what she had to say. When she got really specific about this she decided that the situation that she wanted this to occur in was when she was talking to someone on the phone and he kept asking for her attention. She wanted him to listen to what she had to say. Even more specifically, she wanted him to be quiet, look relaxed and be happily amusing himself while she spoke to her friend. Similarly, at the end of the conversation, Martha wanted to be feeling happy and relaxed, and saying to herself how good little Ben was while she was on the phone.

John wanted to feel that he had really communicated on the same wavelength as his teenage daughter. Specifically, he wanted this to be during their chats about her school progress. At the end of the communication, John wanted to feel really happy inside and to see that he had made his daughter feel comfortable and supported and that the whole conversation was a success. He thought that he would be able to see her smiling and that she might even give him a hug at the end of the conversation.

Lisa knew very clearly that she wanted her eldest child of 10 to turn off the television when she asked him to, first go. She imagined that he would be doing this willingly without a lot of grizzling and whingeing. She would look satisfied and be saying to herself what a cooperative boy he was. Lisa also thought that it would be a huge challenge to really make her scenario come true.

So you see just how specific we need to be in setting our outcomes. It is only by setting our outcomes that we will know for sure that we have achieved them. This is the second step in achieving a successful win–win communication.

So now that you understand what outcome setting is all about, go ahead and write down the answers to the following questions: If you had an outcome that you wanted to achieve with a particular individual in your family life what would that outcome be? What situation would you like that outcome to occur in? How do you want things to turn out, specifically? That is, at the end of the communication, how do you want to look, feel and be talking to yourself about the result that you've produced? How do you want the other person to look, feel and talk at the end of the communication?

How to Build Rapport, and the Issue of Trust

The third step is to build rapport. We all could do with a good dose of learning to build rapport. If you think there are many areas in your life where this could be useful, you're right. Imagine how much easier life would be at work if we had rapport with our staff, bosses, colleagues and customers. Not to mention how much more rewarding our relationships with our spouses or partners would be if we could just reduce the differences between them and us and feel like we're communicating on the same wavelength. When we reduce the differences between ourselves and others and we build rapport, it feels like we're talking to our very best friend whom we've known for years. That's how dramatic the response is.

In order to learn how to build rapport we first need to be aware of how we're currently doing or not doing 'our rapport'. So next time you ask your eight-year-old to turn off the television, just notice how you do or do not build rapport. Where do you stand when you ask him to turn off the television, or do you sit down to do the deed? What does your body language say to him when you communicate? What are you saying with your facial expression before you even open your mouth to speak?

Do you ask him in the middle of chopping the vegetables, doing your tax return or talking on the telephone to Aunt Patricia? What underlying message are you sending to your child about the importance of turning off the television when you are so engrossed in your own activities? So engrossed that you can't take the time to build a little rapport first and then ask him to turn off the television. This is where I often hear parents groaning and saying, well that's too hard. Why should I have to bother with building rapport? They're my kids and because they're my kids they should listen to me just because I'm their parent. Wow! Where did that come from? It sounds like a hangover from those early days of parenting where 'children should be seen and not heard', 'Do it now because I said so' and 'Wait till your father gets home'. Would you expect your colleague to do something straightaway just because you told her to? Would you expect your best friend to do something straightaway just because you told her to? Would you even treat your best friend like that? So why would you treat your child like that? Why do we find it so difficult to afford our children the same amount of respect that we afford our friends? It's simply a matter of old conditioning. That's how it's always been and so that's how it should be done. Well, not to my mind it shouldn't.

The world is an ever-evolving place and things are changing all the time. The only thing that doesn't seem to have changed is the way we treat and communicate with our children. It's time that we caught up. It's time that we started affording our children the time that they deserve.

In this whole area of communicating with children and parenting them, most parents fight constantly against the all-time greatest enemy — *time*. For most human beings, time is a big issue. Many parents feel that they have to be doing 10 things at once or nothing will ever get done. Grandfather time is the greatest time waster, however, when it comes to building rapport with your children.

He whispers in your ear that you have to get dinner on the table by 7.00 pm. He tells you that if you do a number of things at once then maybe, just maybe, you might get 10 whole minutes to yourself in peace. Well, just imagine how blissful it might feel to be sitting on the lounge with your feet up, having a drink, and as you're imagining that, go a little further and imagine how you will feel when you have all of that blissful time because there is *no* family to share it with.

You didn't have any time for them and pretty soon they found that they didn't have any time for you. You didn't take the time to establish a relationship with your children because you were always too busy peeling those vegetables or doing that tax return, or racing to get things done to have that 10 minutes of peace and quiet. When all is said and done, it's simply a matter of values. The things that we spend our precious time on are the things that we value the most.

So let me ask you a very important question. How much do you value your relationship with your children? Enough to learn a few simple skills that will make them feel like you're communicating on their wavelength? Enough to practise those skills in each area of your life with your family and perhaps even out and beyond into the world of business and friends?

In truth, establishing rapport is the most simple skill in the world to learn. It's just a matter of practice. And practice, like everything else, takes a little time. The good news is that in building rapport you are more than likely going to make your life a whole lot easier and you just might save yourself some of that precious commodity — *time*. How would you feel if your 10-year-old were to go and clean up his room with a minimum of fuss? How would life be if your three-year-old packed up his Lego the very first time that you asked him to? 'Impossible!' I hear you say. 'Can't be done,' I hear you murmur. 'Prove it,' says another voice. And I intend to. The secret is all in the rapport.

When it comes to building rapport, our non-verbals or non-language, are a highly important factor. The very way in which we sit or stand communicates something. The way in which we breathe and the pace at which we speak communicates many things to our listener. The tone of voice and the pitch level of our voice also communicates a great deal about the mood that we are in. In short, you cannot not communicate. The verbal component of our language, the words that we use, are in many respects the icing on the cake. Imagine this scenario if you will.

Young Tom has just kicked his mum's best vase over with his football. He was told not to kick the football in the house. Tom's mother is standing in the hallway with her arms crossed, her lips pursed and her body rigid. Her breathing is rapid and shallow and her facial expression consists of a serious frown. Now, do you need to know the words that she will say to Tom to know what her communication will be about? No. The body language says it all. Imagine this next scenario.

Nicola has just brought home her school report and she is showing it to her father. Her father is now looking at the report. Nicola hasn't seen the report herself, but she can tell by her father's non-verbals what the results are. Her father's body is relaxed and his breathing is deep and slow. He has a very happy smile on his face and his eyes glisten with what can only be interpreted as pride. Do you think that Nicola needs to see the report to know how she went? Do you think she needs to see the report to know how her father feels about her results? No. Nicola's father's non-verbals are very strong.

Every second of every moment of every day we are communicating. If we breathe, we communicate. If we move our body or keep it still, we communicate. If we move the muscles in our face or not, we still communicate.

With every non-verbal we can't help but communicate a message to others. With every non-verbal we have the opportunity to build rapport with our kids, our partners, our colleagues and our friends.

In order to learn how to build rapport in a different way, an improved way, you have to be willing to take the risk of making a change, a change in the way in which you relate to others. When we change the way we communicate with others we change not only our relationship to them but also our relationship to ourselves. That can be pretty scary. Some people ask, 'If I change my relationship to myself then I'm changing *me*. If I change *me*, who will I be?' The answer to that: someone with greater knowledge and insight into themselves plus improved communication skills.

For many people, change can be very frightening. Remember the saying 'Better the devil you know than the devil you don't know'. Well, many of us feel that way about making any kind of changes in our lives, no matter how small they might be.

There is a risk involved. But if you could be shown just how easy it is to build rapport in a simple three-step procedure that may be different from how you already do it, would you be willing to take the risk of changing? If the answer is *yes*, read on.

Let's look at the beginning of building rapport. The very next time you talk to someone, anyone at home, at work or out shopping, notice how they are standing or sitting and go ahead and sit or stand in that way too. Good, that's the beginning of building rapport.

Once you can sit or stand in a similar position to another person, notice what happens if you actually look them in the eye. Don't stare at them like you're burning a hole in their forehead, just look at them easily, and actually look into their eyes. For some of us, making eye contact with someone can be pretty scary, even when it's a helpless (or not so helpless) three-year-old. You can just imagine the panic that sets in when I get people on the Talking with Kids workshops to do this exercise. For many of them it is the first real contact they have made with anyone in a long time. During the workshop program they are often asked to do this in pairs and with a total stranger. It usually is a BFO (blinding flash of the obvious) for many of them when they realise just how little they take the time to make contact and build rapport with others.

Now that you can sit or stand in a similar manner and actually make eye contact, see if you can breathe at a similar rate to the other person. This might sound crazy, but it really works. It's an incredible way to build rapport. And don't think for one minute that the person is going to know what you're doing. Well, not unless you make it really obvious. Take your time, relax. Sit in a similar position, breathe at the same pace as them, and look them in the eyes. If you do this, you will have a much better chance of getting their attention. This is how quick and simple it is to build rapport.

So instead of calling to your child from the kitchen to turn off the television, while you are peeling the vegetables at the same time as looking for that sharper knife in the bottom drawer, just try a little rapport building. Put down the vegetable, go into the loungeroom and sit directly in front of your child, relax, breathe, look him in the eye and say, 'I want you to turn off the television now'. Try it. Go on. Even if it's just to see what happens. It's worth the effort because then he can't pretend that he didn't hear you (remember selective listening!) and he gets a clear congruent message that says 'Please do this now' instead of you having to yell it from a distance, goodness knows how many times.

I suggest that you work on building rapport at every possible opportunity. You will be amazed at the difference it makes in how you relate to others. You will also experience a change in how you relate to yourself, especially when you start to see the results of your efforts at rapport building.

Now that we are more familiar with the first two steps in our procedure, that is to say, know your outcome and building rapport, let's look at the next step — active listening.

Active Listening

Has there ever been a time in your life when you just wanted someone to listen to you? A time when you just wanted your point of view to be heard? When you went to your friend, partner or parent with the problem, what did they do?

Let's look at some typical examples of non-active listening to highlight the importance of active listening.

Judy had just lost her job at the bank and, needless to say, she was very upset. She rang her best friend Helen and asked her to meet her for a cup of coffee. Helen arrived and Judy began to tell her about losing her job and what it meant to her in her life. Well, no sooner had she said two sentences when Helen interrupted her and started talking about when she lost her job and how distraught she was. Helen went on and on about her own personal history. Judy felt disappointed and was angry that Helen couldn't even hear her out on what she had to say without interrupting and talking about herself.

Peter was having some difficulty in building up enough business to pay his rent and other expenditures. He decided to go to Sam and talk it over with him, as Sam had at one point been in a similar position. So Peter organised a meeting with Sam at a place and time that was mutually convenient. Sam turned up late and proceeded to tell Peter about all the mistakes he had made and what he should be doing with his life and his business. Peter was not impressed. In fact, Peter felt angry at the lack of empathy and sensitivity that Sam showed.

Do you identify with any of these scenarios? Sometimes listening, really listening, to someone can be a very difficult task. Often when we are listening to someone we are not really there, instead we are pretending to listen. Sometimes we aren't listening because we are preparing our reply as the other person is speaking. It is so tempting to diagnose and advise when someone comes to us with a problem. In fact, what the person may really need is someone who is skilled at active listening.

When that someone who comes to us is our own child, it's really difficult not to give advice and offer solutions. Some of us can't help ourselves, we have to tell them what they *should* have done.

Mrs S, a highly capable and intelligent mother of four, confessed to the other parents at the workshop, 'I now realise how ingrained my habit is of giving my children advice. I'm not sure that I can change because I know that I do it with my husband and my friends as well'.

My reply to that is, 'Yes, yes. You can change any habit, it just takes work and a little patience'. Parents who seriously give it a go will find that the rewards are well worth the effort. They will very rapidly notice the difference in their relationship with their children.

The most effective time to use active listening is when your child reveals that he has a problem. Usually you'll be able to spot this by the way the child is showing his feelings. Sometimes it takes a little practice to get used to recognising the warning signals.

Active listening is most appropriate when the child does what I call 'owns the problem'. It helps the child find solutions to his own problem. When the child 'owns the problem' his behaviour is causing problems only to himself and not to his parents. Active listening isn't useful when the child's behaviour is causing the parents to have problems. The sorts of problems that are 'owned by the child' are:

- Annie is feeling sad because she didn't get the lead in the school play.
- Tommy is feeling rejected by his best friend.
- Ruth is feeling angry because she can't decide what subjects to choose for her final year of school.
- Peter is suspended for two days for wagging school.
- Connie is having difficulties in doing her homework.
- Katie is feeling shy because she's tall for her age.
- Rick is doing badly at French because he hates his teacher.

It's important to try to remember as parents that your child's disappointments, frustrations, sadness and anger belong to him and not to you. If you can come from the attitude that his problems do not belong to you, you will find that you are far more effective in helping your child deal with any problems that may arise. This concept is one that, from my experience, parents find hard to accept. Most make their children's problems their own. In doing so, they cause themselves a great deal of grief and as a result, can be less effective as counsellors to their children. Because you accept the fact that your child's problem is his problem doesn't mean that you don't care or that you don't want to help. Allowing the child the responsibility of solving his own problem (with your help by active listening), he has a much better chance of maintaining a high level of self-esteem.

From my own experience with children and parents, it is the children who are encouraged to solve their own problems that maintain a good psychological state, and the other children whose parents solve everything for them are the ones who develop emotional problems. Professional counsellors are effective because they trust the child enough to allow him to be guided to his own solution. When parents can learn to separate themselves from the child's problem they, too, can use active listening to help their child, just like the professional counsellor.

Active listening is a very different type of help from what most parents give. It is paradoxical that the use of active listening gives the parent more influence over the child. This is different from the usual type of influence that parents so often try to exert upon their children, simply because their own parents did things exactly the same way.

When it comes to dealing with our children's problems, we often respond typically with one of the patterns outlined below:

- advising
- moralising
- name calling
- offering solutions
- reassuring
- interpreting
- threatening
- ordering
- persuading with logic
- probing
- instructing
- blaming

Let's look at an example of non-active listening:

Katie: Sarah won't let me play with her toys today and I want to play with her Barbie doll. She's a pain. She never let's me play with her Barbie doll any more.
Mum: Well, why don't you play with some other toys? You've got to learn to get along with your friends, Kate (*advising, moralising*).
Katie: But I don't want to play with the other toys. I don't want to play with her any more, either. She's a pain.
Mum: Well, if you go around calling her a pain, I'd say that she probably thinks that you're a pain (*name calling*). Why don't you go and play with Lucy, instead? (*offering solutions*)

Here is how Katie's mother can help her with active listening:

> *Katie*: Sarah won't let me play with her toys today and I want to play with her Barbie doll. She's a pain. She never let's me play with her Barbie dolls any more.
>
> *Mum*: Are you angry with Sarah?
>
> *Katie*: Yes. She's a pain. I never want to play with her again.
>
> *Mum*: Wow, you must be angry with her not to want to play with her ever again!
>
> *Katie*: That's right. But if I don't play with her, I won't have anyone to play with. Lucy's gone to her grandma's place.
>
> *Mum*: You don't want to be left on your own?
>
> *Katie*: No. Mummy, do you think I could take my Barbie doll over to Sarah's. Do you think she might want to swap Barbie dolls and play with mine for a while?
>
> *Mum*: I don't know. But it sounds like a good idea. That way Sarah and you can play together and have some fun.
>
> *Katie*: Bye, Mummy. I'll be back this afternoon, okay?

In the first version, Katie's mother used many of the typical problem-solving patterns that we are tempted to use in our interactions with our children. In the second version, she used active listening. This allowed Katie to trust herself and come to her own resolution of the problem. It removed her anger and allowed her to develop into a good, self-directed problem-solver.

Here is another situation to illustrate how parents typically try to help their children:

> *Marc*: I don't want any dinner tonight.
>
> *Dad*: Come on. Kids your age need to eat regularly, son (*instructing, persuading with logic*).
>
> *Marc*: But I had a huge breakfast and I'm not hungry now.
>
> *Dad*: Well, just come to the table anyway and you can sit with us while we eat (*suggesting*).
>
> *Marc*: I don't want to eat anything.

Dad: What's wrong with you today? You don't seem yourself (*probing*). Well then. No excuses. Get yourself over here and be with the rest of us while we, at least, eat the food your mother has prepared (*ordering, blaming*).

Now here is how the same boy can be helped with active listening:

Marc: I don't want any lunch today.
Dad: You don't feel like eating?
Marc: I feel kind of upset in the stomach. It's sort of in knots.
Dad: Are you feeling worried today?
Marc: Yeah. I guess I feel scared.
Dad: So, what do you think you're scared about, son?
Marc: Well, Sally rang up this morning and she wants to see me tonight. It sounds really serious. I'm worried she's going to want to break up with me.
Dad: You'd hate to have that happen, huh?
Marc: Yeah, I really like her. I'm especially worried cause I think she's gonna go out with Greg. That would be brutal.
Dad: So that's what's really worrying you, the thought that Sally might want to go out with someone else.

In the first version, his father got caught up on Marc's eating problem and failed to go any deeper. In the second version, his father was far more perceptive and his wonderful active listening uncovered the real problem which had nothing to do with eating at all. If Marc and his father had gone further with the conversation, they would have probably come up with a satisfactory solution for Marc's problem with Sally, with the help of active listening.

Most parents have found that as a result of using active listening they can solve even deep-seated problems that their children may have, problems that previously they would have thought solvable only by a professional counsellor. Sometimes the talk with the child may not end in a conclusive or complete way. Sometimes it is necessary for the child to go away and solve the problem for himself.

Just a little active listening from the parent can, however, start the chain of events that leads to a solution.

Once parents know that many sessions with professional counsellors end on an incomplete note, only to see the client return to the next session with the problem solved, they can rest more easily about their own use of active listening.

Sometimes active listening can be used to help a child accept a situation that isn't pleasant, but one that can't be changed. With active listening, the child is given the chance to express his feelings and often that is enough. Most children just want to know that there will always be someone there for them and that they can express their feelings and that these feelings will be accepted. When a child hurts itself, the typical response of a parent is to soothe the the child and say 'It will feel better' or 'You didn't hurt yourself that much'. Many parents respond with, 'Don't be a baby. Be a man and stop that crying right this minute'.

When a child has hurt himself he needs to be told that his feelings are valid. This can be done easily using active listening.

> *Veronica*: Mummy, I fell over and I'm bleeding. Ooooo. It really hurts.
> *Mum*: It really hurts? You fell over and hurt your knee?
> *Veronica*: Yes, look how bad I hurt it. Look, it's bleeding.
> *Mum*: I can see you've hurt it pretty badly. It is bleeding.
> *Veronica: (stops crying)* Mummy, will you put something on it?
> *Mum*: Of course, darling. Let's get some ice to cool it down and then we'll get a sticking plaster for you.

In this case, the mother didn't deny the child's feelings and didn't make the problem her own. Most importantly, she didn't make the child feel bad or guilty about crying or expressing any of her feelings.

Many parents in the workshops find that when a child is hurt and active listening is employed the child often stops crying fairly quickly. It seems that the most important thing for the child is to know that his feelings are being understood by his parents.

Even when a child is whingeing, active listening can be used. It's difficult for any parent to cope with a whingeing child without feeling frustrated and angry. The trick is to accept the way that the child is feeling instead of trying to get rid of the whingeing and pestering by reassuring the child or threatening him. Let's look at an example.

Martha's three-year-old was crying because she was going out and leaving him with a baby-sitter. As Martha hadn't been out anywhere in almost a year, it was difficult for her to keep her cool and not get angry with Tod, which Martha admits was her usual way of coping with most of Tod's behaviour. Instead, the scenario went something like this:

> *Tod*: Don't go, Mum. Don't go (*crying*).
> *Martha*: (*resisting the urge to get angry*) You'll miss me, Tod. I know, sweetheart. Mum will miss you, too.
> *Tod*: Mummy, I'll miss you.
> *Martha*: I know, Tod. Mum will miss you, too. Just like you miss Mum.

Once Tod's feelings were acknowledged, he stopped crying and started chatting with the baby-sitter.

One of the more exciting and unusual uses of active listening is to encourage a child's intellectual development. Sometimes as parents or teachers we have a strong investment in the child thinking and having the same opinions that we have. If we use active listening to discuss a topic with a child, we're actually stimulating his ability to think for himself, which is a far more useful skill to have in life than just adopting someone else's opinion.

As parents and teachers we need to ask ourselves some serious questions. Some of which I'd like you to consider right now:

- Can you tolerate your child having a different opinion from you?
- Can you tolerate your child having different values from you?

145

- How do you feel when your child expresses an opinion that is different from your own?
- Can you remember ever having strange perspectives on life when you were a kid?
- How difficult is it for you to let your child just sit with and grapple with a problem instead of you having to come in and rescue him?
- How do you feel about teaching your child to be independent?

The answers to all of these questions are very significant in that they reflect the sort of relationship that a child has with his parents or teacher.

When parents in the workshops take the risk of biting their tongues and truly listening to what their children have to say, they are often astounded by the insights and the brilliance that their children display. This is why I feel that children are our greatest teachers. The respect that they deserve has, in my personal opinion, been denied them for many years all because of an old-fashioned attitude to parenting that only now is slowly changing. Parents wonder why there is a generation gap and why their teenagers start to rebel when they get to a certain age.

If parents and teachers could learn to listen more instead of responding in the old ways of reprimanding, admonishing, threatening and blaming, their children would feel safe to express their feelings and really talk with their parents so that those barriers of miscommunication are prevented from building up.

Like most extremely effective tools, active listening can be damaging if used incorrectly. To help you avoid the pitfalls that may occur when you use active listening, I thought it might be useful to highlight common mistakes that parents and teachers make when they first begin to use the technique. Of course, everyone will differ in the ease with which they use active listening and you may not experience any of the pitfalls described here.

The first trap that some parents fall into in using active listening is to open the doors of communication but to close them prematurely before the child has finished with his communication. Sometimes the parent says to the child, 'Tell me everything', and then shuts the door as soon as they hear something they didn't want to hear. The parent doesn't continue to actively listen long enough for the child to say what he needs to say. Let's look at this a little more closely:

Julie: Mummy, Tania took my Barbie doll and then she pushed me over.
Mum: You didn't like her taking your Barbie doll and pushing you?
Julie: I'm gonna get her Barbie doll and throw it in the garbage and then I'm gonna hit her back.
Mum: Two wrongs don't make a right, Julie (*moralising*).
Julie: I don't care. I just want to hit her.
Mum: Fighting is not ladylike and never solves the problem, Julie (*moralising*).

Parents who begin to actively listen and then take the information that is given and turn it around so that they moralise, judge or advise, teach their children that it isn't safe to give information.

Another trap that's easy to fall into when first using active listening is that of parroting back to the child what he says instead of paraphrasing it. The child is likely to just look at you and say, 'Dad, why are you copying everything I'm saying?' Keep in mind that the words the child uses are just a vehicle to express how he feels. As a parent you need to start reading between the lines. It takes practice for parents to learn how to feed back messages to their children that contain the hidden message and not the parroted message.

Sometimes a parent will use the skill of active listening to manipulate their child into doing what they want him to do or thinking the way they want him to think. For example:

> *Jamie*: Boy, I hate that creep Joe.
> *Mum*: You think that Joe is a creep?
> *Jamie*: I sure do. Every time I start a game he takes over. So I just give it right back to him and I take over. But it means that we're not real good friends any more. Now that he's acting like such a jerk.
> *Mum*: So you're learning that two wrongs don't make a right (*Mum sends her own message here*).
> *Jamie*: No, I'm learning what a jerk he is. He just takes over everything. I never get a word in edgewise.
> *Mum*: So you're learning that communicating is a two-way street. You need to take turns (*Again Mum is sending her own message and interpreting Jamie's response incorrectly*).
> *Jamie*: No, I want us to be friends again. Oh, it doesn't matter. Don't worry about it, Mum. I'll just punch him in the head again.

You can see from this example how Jamie's mother is misinterpreting his messages. She starts by paraphrasing but fails to continue the process or offer any window statements that will encourage Jamie to open up. In fact, she doesn't really want him to open up. Instead, she wants him to get her message about how she wants him to behave around his friends. No wonder Jamie gives up. He was quick to sense his mother's intentions. Instead of steering him in the right direction, she is threatening his way of thinking and insisting on having her hand on the steering wheel the whole time. Most children become fearful of this form of control because it threatens their independence. Active listening is not a technique for parent-directed change. Those of you who think that it is will immediately start sending your own biases and your own personal messages and you will not be encouraging your child either to communicate freely with you or to generate his own solutions to his problems.

Sometimes a parent will actively listen but without any empathy. This is a trap parents fall into when they try to actively listen straight from a book without sitting down and practising first with their partner or friend. They jump in and use a textbook-style technique on their child, which lets the child know that they *don't* understand their feelings. Essentially, in the use of active listening the parent's outcome is to open the window for communication to occur and to feed back accurately to the child his feelings about the situation at hand.

Feelings, as we have seen in Chapter 6, can be fairly scary things for parents to deal with. They can't deal with their children's feelings because they can't deal with their own feelings. It's all too hard and so much easier to sweep it all under the carpet. Many of us were raised in a way that said 'It's not right, it's not polite and it's incredibly weak to show your feelings. So don't do it'.

No wonder we need to practise feeding back feelings to our kids in our active listening. Dealing with feelings is not something that we are necessarily used to or are very confident about. Many of us would prefer to leave that to the professionals. It's a case of fear of the unknown. If we want to learn to actively listen and really communicate with our children, we need to acknowledge that we have feelings and that they have feelings. By starting to use active listening, parents begin to realise that feelings aren't dangerous or pathological but just a part of life.

Of course there are times when children don't want to talk about their feelings, and in this case, active listening is really inappropriate. There will also be occasions when you simply just don't have the time to devote to allowing your child to express all his feelings. In this case, active listening is also inappropriate. If you don't have the time to get into it, then don't. Make an appropriate time to talk about it later. A time when your child can easily release all of his feelings, knowing you're not about to rush out the door.

Sometimes your children don't want active listening, they just want some information or some practical help. Once again, we need to be clear that active listening is for when a child 'owns a problem' and is expressing some feeling about the problem. When your child asks you to drive him to the shops, he is clearly not in need of active listening and you would cause major frustration by initiating it in this case. It's not only important to be able to know when to use active listening, it's also important to know when to stop using it. When you child has had enough he will probably indicate this to you by some comment or by getting physically restless. Even though you may feel that the problem is not yet solved, it's important to back off when you get these sorts of signals. Just leave the window open for more discussion if he needs it.

Well, you may be thinking that active listening sounds pretty complicated or you may be itching to try it with your friends and your partner and your children. Either way, it must be clear to you by now that knowing your outcome, appealing to your child's values and building rapport with him are just the beginning and that, in fact, active listening is what the success or failure of your communication will depend upon if and when your child expresses a problem. The good thing about active listening is that when you start to use it with your children and they truly understand that you're there to listen to them, it's amazing how much better they become at listening to your needs. Active listening has been known to turn poor relationships around permanently. It's not the total answer, as you still need to focus on building rapport and respecting the other person's values, but active listening can sure make the difference that makes the difference.

Active Listening with the Very Young Child

So how to you use active listening with children who are very young and who don't have much verbal communication? Well, cast your mind back to Chapter 2 where we discussed just how early communication begins between you and your child and remember that even if your child isn't communicating verbally yet, he is still communicating non-verbally. If your child can communicate with you non-verbally, then you can use active listening which results in him getting his needs met. Allow me to explain.

When a baby cries, a mother responds to that cry by picking him up because she interprets his crying as the need for a cuddle. If the mother is actively listening to her child's non-verbal message she will realise that if he continues to cry then she has misinterpreted his feelings and that she needs to try something else. The mother then covers the child with a blanket thinking that he may be cold. When he continues to cry, if she is actively listening the mother will take another tack and she might give the baby a bottle. If the baby stops crying and she is actively listening, then she will know that she has accurately interpreted the baby's feelings. The baby has communicated to the mother through non-verbal messages and the mother has met the baby's needs through non-verbal means. This, too, is a form of active listening. The baby has a problem and the mother is interpreting the message and trying to feed it back to the baby to see if she is accurate or not. If parents became more skilled at active listening and meeting their baby's needs, then there would be little need to listen to the advice of so-called experts. Instead, the parents would be highly skilled in interpreting what their child needs at any given moment rather than going 'by the book'. The parents of very young children need to actively listen for long enough until they pinpoint the area of need, just as the parents of older children listen long enough for the child to fully express his feelings.

The same technique can be employed with toddlers. For example, if Phoebe stands in her playpen and starts to cry loudly, her mother might come over and hand her a teddy bear. If Phoebe throws the teddy bear out of the playpen and her mother picks it up again and gives it back to her saying 'If you throw it out again, I won't pick it up for you', she may be misinterpreting Phoebe's feelings through a lack of active listening. Phoebe may start to cry even louder as a result of this lack of active listening and a lack of meeting her needs. The amount of time that a parent spends with an infant or toddler certainly affects the child's development through the early years. It seems to me that the important factor is more that through spending time with the child, the parent becomes more attuned to his needs and more effective at using active listening to meet these needs, either verbally or non-verbally.

Congruency

Congruency occurs when what you think, feel, say and do all match up together. How many times have you said 'yes' when you really wanted to say 'no'? How many times have you pretended that you knew something when you didn't? How many times have you pretended not to be upset by something when you were? As I have mentioned to you before, children have a real instinct for anything that is incongruent. They seem to know when you're lying, even if it's a white lie. The most effective means of communicating with them is to be congruent.

So how do you know if you're being congruent or not? You know by the child's reaction. If you know your outcome and you build rapport with your child and even appeal to his values but he doesn't respond, then you need to check your level of congruency. It may be that you have asked him to turn off the television with a voice that really says 'I know you're not going to do this for me'. If you want him to really get the message that you want the television off then you need to go up to him and let your body language and your voice communicate the importance of this request.

Don't wring your hands, stand on one foot and look sheepishly at him with a hopeful sound in your voice. Be congruent. Stand in front of the television, look him in the eye, take your time to breathe and then say calmly and firmly, 'Turn the television off now please'. This way, not only will you be congruent, but you will come away from the situation feeling far more powerful and effective as a parent than you would if you had chosen the first style of communication. Children just know when you mean what you say. Make them hear you the first time by building rapport with them and by being congruent. It is the parents who have difficulty in being congruent that become frustrated and end up resorting to threats and verbal abuse. Don't get hung-up on the thought that by appealing to their values you need to sweet-talk them, because you don't. You are simply providing them with what they value. There's no reason why you can't make a statement that appeals to their values and state it in a powerful and highly congruent manner. There's nothing stopping you but a little practice.

I have found over the years that parents are amazed at the difference in their child's reaction when they are congruent with him. Being congruent communicates to your child the importance of what you are saying, and it's really just a matter of being aware of how you say things with both your body and your voice. Remember to make sure that your body language matches your voice, because being congruent is essentially a non-verbal activity and the child gets most of his information from the visuals that you present to him. The best way that parents on the Talking with Kids program found to become truly congruent was to practise their congruency on a friend or a partner before trying it out on their children. Most people found it so easy that they combined it quickly with the other win–win communication steps and began to use them almost immediately on their children. The hardest step was taking the plunge and doing it, trying it and seeing how it worked. When a parent is congruent, the child notices the change in his parent's attitude but he doesn't see it as an aggressive change because his parent is actually being more honest with him and treating him with more respect.

We have now looked at the benefits of appealing to your child's values, taking the time to build rapport, doing this congruently and with active listening when appropriate. These are all highly useful skills to have, but without the final step of our six-step action plan the entire process would not be complete.

The Win–Win Method with Kids

What do you do when the problem at hand is not one that the child owns but instead is a conflict between yourself and the child? Most parents choose the win–lose method or the lose–win method, as we discussed in Chapter 3, or they use a combination of these two to deal with a conflict situation. But what if you had available to you a third alternative that was easy to use and you could use it on the spot at the time that the conflict arises? The win–win method or conflict resolution method is one that brings a sigh of relief to every parent on the Talking with Kids workshop. This is not a new technique. In fact, many people have been using the technique of conflict resolution in the workplace for years but have never thought of using it with their families.

Legal conflicts, marital disagreements and industrial disputes can all be resolved using the win–win process, and therefore, so can any conflict between yourself and your child. This win–win method requires that all individuals concerned possess equal power and that is why it has not been customary to use it in dealing with children.

If you want to afford your children the respect that you would afford your marital partner, your best friend or your business partner, then the win–win method is a useful technique for you to use. This method is a non-power method, unlike the win–lose or lose–win methods. This third alternative is win–win because the solution to the problem must be acceptable to both parties. For example, when there is a conflict of needs between the parent and the child, the parent asks the child to participate with her in a joint effort to search for a solution acceptable to both of them. Either the parent or the child or both together may come up with the final solution that is used. All suggestions are considered equally. Both the child and the adult evaluate the selection of solutions and make a final decision on which alternative would work for both of them. There is no hard sell, no power struggle, and no coercion, as each party accepts the chosen solution fully. Neither party resists the decision.

The win–win method does not involve coming up with stock ways to deal with a range of typical family conflict situations, such as tidying bedrooms, completing chores, doing homework and getting ready for school. This method encourages both the child and the parent to develop a solution to creatively develop a solution that is best for them. Each family will no doubt come up with different solutions to the same conflict situation. If parents employ this win–win method then the future of effective parenting is assured. When parents combine the use of all six techniques in this chapter, then I believe that the future of *excellence* in parenting is assured.

First, let's look at some of the reasons why the win–win method is so effective in achieving a positive outcome in parent–child conflicts.

When the solution involves the child's input, he is highly motivated to carry out the decision made. This high level of motivation does not occur when a child has a decision imposed on him. Parents usually find when they do this that they have to nag and remind and argue to get their decision carried out. No so with the win–win method. The child gets a feeling that the decision has been his as well and he therefore makes a greater commitment to carrying it out. The child also responds favourably to the fact that his parents

155

have not tried to win at the expense of him losing.

Another advantage of using the win–win method is that the sorts of solutions that come out of using this method are often more creative and of a much better quality than the solutions that either the child or the parent may have come up with on their own. It is also a method that encourages your child's thinking skills. This is a method of problem-solving that actually brings you and your child closer together. When you use the win–win method, you eliminate any need to use power over each other and you use a lot less time and energy because you don't have to reinforce any decision that's been made. The win–win method's greatest advantage is that it is truly a problem-solving process because it allows the parent and the child to get down to the nitty-gritty of the behaviour or situation that's causing the problem. In a sense, it is almost therapeutic in itself as it often brings about the sort of changes that would occur if an individual were to have professional intervention.

How's that for a money-saving effective option? Wouldn't you rather do things in a less costly, less time-consuming, less energy-consuming, more effective manner that actually works? You may be surprised to know that not all parents answer yes to this question.

Some parents are very resistant to using the win–win method. They have totally understandable fears and concerns about using the method. They often believe that it sounds great in theory but are sceptical about its use in practice. One of the major concerns of parents in using the win–win method is that they equate it to giving in and being weak. This is because so many of us are used to thinking about conflicts in win–lose terms, that someone must win and someone must lose. Unlike the lose–win method, the child doesn't get his way at the expense of the parent. In the win–win method the parent gets her needs met too, and she too has to accept completely the outcome decided upon.

Even though the win–win method often involves only one or two family members and not the whole family, some parents see it as a 'family meeting' type of activity that their parents tried to use on them. In the family meeting the parents had already decided upon the outcome and they gathered the children together to educate them as to this chosen outcome. The win–win method isn't anything like this, since the outcome is created by every group member at the time of the get-together. The outcome must be acceptable to *all* group members. There is also the belief which we've all grown up with that says there has to be a leader in a group, someone has to take charge and make the final decision. Otherwise the discussion will just go round and round in circles and we will never reach an outcome. This is not true; it's just a belief that we've grown up with because that's how decisions were made at home and at school and often at work. In the win–win method you may decide to have someone open the discussion and lead it by writing down all the suggestions on a piece of paper, but this in no way suggests that this person or any other makes the final decision on their own.

The biggest objection of all to using the win–win method is that parents think that it will be too time consuming. The time that it will take to come up with a solution usually depends upon the type of problem and the willingness of the children and the parents creatively to come up with an outcome that suits everyone. Of course, when you first start using the win–win method, you may need a little more time just because you're not used to doing things this way. The win–win method saves a lot of time in the long run and some parents at the Talking With Kids workshops reported that after using the win–win method for a couple of months they found that problems didn't come up as often because the family had already worked through all of the major concerns, such as pocket money, doing chores, getting out of bed on time, tidying up rooms and the use of the television. The little problems that came up were also dealt with on the spot with a minimum of time and fuss, because everyone had become accustomed to using the new technique and really enjoyed using it. When the win–win method is first used with older children who have been dealt with using the win–lose method, then it may take a little bit longer because of the lack of trust already created by the use of that method. The parents need to prove to their children that this is not just some new psychological method that they are going to use to get their own way once again.

Sometimes there are parents who feel that because they are brighter, wiser, older and more experienced, they are justified in using the win–lose method and therefore using power over their children. Many parents believe that they are totally justified in doing this, and it is the most difficult belief to change in an adult. They believe that it is their god-given right to control their children with power. There is no doubt that parents are older and probably wiser, but when I ask parents on the workshops whether they were happy with all the decisions that their parents made for them, they say no. Children are innately wise in knowing how they feel and what they want. The win–win method takes advantage of both the child's and the parent's wisdom to come up with solutions to problems.

The final objection that parents have against the use of the win–win method is that it's fine with older children who can communicate and reason things out, but it can't possibly work with a preschooler, or even worse, a baby. Remember that active listening can be used on a baby. And it's the same for the win–win method. The parent has to be skilled at noticing the child's non-verbal signals and she may have to do most of the talking, but believe me, it can work, and work very successfully.

Before we move onto learning how to use the win–win method, I'd just like to say that there are times when the win–win method may not be your final choice of action, but I would always try to use it wherever possible. For example, if your three-year-old runs out into the traffic you are probably not going to sit him down and have a long conversation about road safety. You're probably going to use the win–lose method to ensure that he doesn't run out into the traffic again. However, you could also use the win–win method to find out why he ran out into the traffic and how he could have those needs met in another way that wouldn't endanger his safety. For example, some children run out into the traffic because they are fascinated by cars. You could sit him down and tell him all the good things and the dangerous things about cars. Then you could take him outside and together agree on a boundary where he can be safe and still look at the fascinating cars going by. I always try to use the win–win method, even when I use some aspect of the win–lose method, because at least then the child still feels like he has some control and some input into what's going on.

So now let's go ahead and see just how easy it is to use this method of resolving conflicts.

Step 1 What's the problem? This is one of the most important steps in the win–win process. You need to get the child's attention and get him involved by securing his willingness to solve the problem. For some parents this is the only stumbling block they come up against. Once they get their child's cooperation to participate, the process usually flows smoothly. To make life easy for yourself, it's best to choose a time when your child isn't busy doing other things. This way he won't resent being interrupted.

Sit the child down and state clearly that there is a problem and that you need his help to solve it so that both of you can get what you want. Always state the problem from an 'I' perspective, which means that you avoid blaming or putting the child down. For example, say, 'When you do this I feel this way...' The use of 'I' statements not only avoids blame but lets your child know that you're taking responsibility for how you feel.

Be very clear that you want your child to join you in solving the problem to your mutual satisfaction. Spell out clearly that the name of the game is win–win. Tell him, 'If you don't win, then I don't win'. Get his agreement to problem solve with you.

Step 2 Now we brainstorm and generate a number of possible solutions. Try to get your child's ideas first before contributing your own. If possible, write these down on a big piece of paper stuck on the wall with blue tack. This takes 10 seconds to set up and makes it easier for all parties to see the possibilities (if they're old enough to read). If it is not possible to set this up, then write the ideas down as best you can. All suggestions are to be accepted. Do not comment yet on any of the suggestions made or you will stop the process in its tracks. Keep pressing for ideas until it's clear that you have enough to work with or that there are no more ideas forthcoming.

Step 3 Now that you have both contributed ideas, you can start evaluating them. You might start by saying, 'Which of these solutions do you like the best?' Gradually narrow down the solutions together by eliminating ones that don't work or by circling the ones you both think will work. Be honest here about how you feel and say if you don't think you'd be happy with one of the alternatives.

Step 4 Make a final decision. If both parties have been open and honest, you will probably find that you can easily choose the best alternative together. Keep asking the child, 'Do you think that this one would solve our problem?' Avoid making the final choice seem as though it is set in concrete. Rather, suggest that you will both agree to go with one particular idea and see if that works out. If it doesn't, you will agree to meet again to find a better solution. Make sure that when you both choose an option that you both commit to making that option work as best you can. Each person has to agree to keep their part of the bargain.

Step 5 Now together make the decision of who is to do what and when you are to start doing these things. Here is your chance to get really specific on what is required. The more specific you both get then the greater the chance of this option working. Only go on to Step 5 when it is clear that both parties have agreed to go with a certain solution. To carry out this solution you may have to buy certain things or qualify certain things. For example, if the issue is about cleaning up the bedroom, then you have to agree on what is considered clean. If the issue is about who does what chores, then you may wish to buy a small whiteboard on which the chores can be written up and a person's name assigned to each chore. You may also have to set a time and a day when the chore has to be completed. The next chapter on teaching your children values will give you some great ideas on how to implement your ideas, but first let's look at the final step in the win–win method.

Step 6 Since not all decisions will turn out to be useful ones, you need to check back with your child to see if he is still happy with the decision and modify the decision accordingly.

Of course, no conflict situation is a textbook case and you may find that the first possibility that you and your child come up with suits you both so that you don't need to brainstorm any other alternatives. Sometimes the final solution will come up in Step 3. Whatever happens will be unique to you and your children and the type of conflict that you need to resolve.

Troubleshooting

Sometimes you will find that you make mistakes when you first start using the win–win method. To help you avoid some of these mistakes, let's discuss possible pitfalls before they occur.

If your child refuses to sit down and discuss the problem, or he just sits there sullenly and refuses to participate in the problem solving, or if he leaves halfway through because he doesn't get it all his way, or if he keeps insisting that it will be like old times where the parents always get their own way, then the best way to handle this resistance is to do one of three things. Firstly, forget momentarily about the win–win method and just start actively listening. This in itself will open up doors to future cooperation. Secondly, send your own 'I' messages to him about how you feel regarding his lack of willingness to participate. Remember to own your feelings and not judge or blame him. And thirdly, leave the problem unresolved for a few days and then try again.

If you find that your child is happy to participate but you can't come up with an agreed-upon solution then go back to step 2 and generate more solutions or call a truce and say you will continue resolving the conflict the next day at a prearranged time. Sometimes deeper feelings of resentment about other issues get in the way of solving a particular problem, so the idea is to ask if this is happening and deal with these other issues first.

There is a strong temptation for many parents to revert to their old ways of win–lose control methods if the win–win method becomes difficult at any stage. All I do is encourage you not to fall into this trap. If you revert to the win–lose method your child is likely to feel tricked in some way and become angry with you.

If you find that you go through the steps of the win–win method successfully but at some point your child fails to live up to his commitment, you need to send him 'I' messages about how this makes you feel. Often these slip-ups happen because your child has agreed to something that he finds out later that he simply can't do or he's just not used to being self-disciplined and needs a second chance to succeed. Sometimes your child may forget to live up to his side of the bargain. Other times your child will test you out by not living up to the commitment just to see if you revert to the old ways of punishment and control. By all means confront your child about not living up to his part of the bargain, but do it with those 'I' messages and without shame, blame or threats. Sometimes you need to sit the child down and let him know how important this is to both of you and the well-being of other family members. This is not a game and it will take some degree of work.

A lot of strength and courage is often needed by those parents who are used to employing the 'peace at any price' lose–win method. Their children also find it difficult to use the win–win method because they are so used to simply getting their own way. When these parents realise how rewarding being a parent can be when both they and their children get their needs met, they usually find the strength to continue to use the win–win method.

Other stumbling blocks that might occur are when the child sees that the parents are coming to the discussion with a united parental front. For this reason it is essential that each parent makes it clear that they are representing their own individual needs in the discussion.

Does the Win–Win Method Ever Fail?

At every Talking with Kids workshop the question is always asked, 'Does the win–win method ever fail?' The answer is *yes*! The win–win method fails to work when either the parent is not committed to using the new technique for reasons of fear or a need to retain control. The win–win method fails to work successfully when one parent uses it and the other parent continues to use the win–lose method or the lose–win method. This new technique can fail with older teenagers who have been so used to the win–lose method that they just don't trust their parents enough to try the new method. These children have already 'given their parents the sack' as parents and they are no longer interested in trying to cooperate in any way with their parents. Finally, the win–win method will not be successful if the parents choose to use it with a combination of the win–lose or lose–win methods. Once children are given a taste of the win–win method they often resent their parents' use of the other methods.

However, if the win–win method is used accurately with the full conviction that it will work and with a determination to not give in when the going gets tough, it brings a sense of freedom and joy to the parents and the children that use it.

Key Points

❖ Many of us feel that our children just don't listen to us and that they have a strange disease called 'selective listening'.

❖ Whether we are children or adults, we are usually most interested in topics that are related to us and our values.

❖ There are six major steps in a win–win communication. They are: know your outcome; build rapport; listen actively; be congruent; know the other person's values; and use the win–win technique.

❖ Time is the greatest barrier used to justify not being able to use the win–win approach effectively.

❖ Knowing your outcome means knowing the result you want.

❖ Developing rapport means reducing the differences between you and the other person. You can do this by subtly copying the body language of the other person and by increasing your eye contact with them.

❖ Active listening means listening to your child and feeding back to him the emotional content behind his communication. You do this to see if your interpretation is correct. If it was incorrect, simply try again. You should only use active listening when the problem that the child has does not directly affect you. The child needs to 'own' his own problem. It is paradoxical to use active listening if it gives more power to the parent.

❖ If you accept that your child's problem is his own problem and not yours, it does not mean that you don't care. Allowing your child to solve his own problem with the help of your active listening gives him a much better chance of maintaining a high level of self-esteem.

❖ When parents can learn to separate themselves from their child's problem, then they can be as effective in helping their child as any professional counsellor.

❖ When it comes to dealing with our children's problems, we often respond with one of the following patterns: advising, moralising, name calling, offering solutions, reassuring, interpreting, threatening, ordering, persuading with logic, probing, instructing, and blaming.

❖ Active listening encourages a child's intellectual development because it stimulates his ability to think for himself.

❖ Like most extremely effective tools, active listening can be damaging if used incorrectly. Some classic pitfalls occur when parents use active listening to manipulate or if they just echo their child's statement. Some parents open the door to communication, but when they hear something they don't like, immediately shut it again.

❖ Congruency means that what you feel, think, say and do all match up.

❖ A win–win outcome means that all individuals are treated equally and with respect and that the outcome achieved pleases everyone involved.

❖ When we change the way in which we communicate with others, we change not only our relationship with them but our relationship with ourselves.

❖ Appealing to someone's set of values will motivate them to help you to achieve your desired outcome.

CHAPTER EIGHT

How to Communicate Values to Your Children

Values are the things that we hold most dear. They are what motivates us and excites us. In many ways, our values run our lives. Children and their parents each have their own sets of values, so what right does a parent have to impose his own values onto his child? The answer is none at all. If we as parents fail to instil some important life values into our children, however, we run the risk of them leading a totally unfocused life where there is little direction and little evidence of them developing into mature and independent adults whose lives work well for them. So we take the track of the lesser of two evils and aim for a balance of allowing our children to keep their own values and giving them some of the values that we consider will help them grow into people that are fully self-expressed.

When it comes to teaching children values, it's not so much of what to teach but how to teach it. Now that you have recorded in writing your five most important values in life, you have some inkling of what sorts of values you might want to teach your children.

As for the 'how', that's where your creativity comes in.

One way of teaching values is by playing games that involve the teaching of the values, games that are fun and exciting and involve the child in learning about these concepts called values. Another very useful method is by the use of allegory. Children love stories, and allegories really bring home to them the positive sides and negative sides of behaviour without being too moralistic. This is especially useful for teenagers who are at the stage where they think they know it all thank you very much and they want to live only by *their* values. By using allegory you can teach them about a certain value without it being too obvious. Reward systems are great for the younger children so that when they demonstrate an understanding and use of the value you are teaching they can get something special or go on a special outing. Whatever method you use, the focus should be on achieving an outcome where the child demonstrates a particular value in some context of her life. The values that I consider the most useful ones to teach to your children are:

- honesty and integrity
- balance and self-discipline
- courage
- peace and win–win
- commitment
- respect
- kindness
- self-reliance and independence
- love
- unselfishness

I suggest that you go easy on yourself and take about four to five weeks to teach each value to your child. You may want to be flexible and spend six weeks on one and four weeks on another. It's totally up to you the format that you wish to use. Maybe you just want to leave it entirely open and see how long it takes to teach each individual value.

How to Compose an Allegory

The value of metaphor lies in the fact that you can choose characters that your children will immediately relate to. You can choose people who you already know your children have as role models, whether it be a film star, rock star, big brother or someone at school.

Another alternative is to choose characters that are very similar to your children in age and in experience. This way you can draw on recent or past events that have actually happened in your family and have your character achieve the desired demonstration of the value. Or it may be that the child has failed to demonstrate good use of the value and the lesson is what did she learn from that and what were the consequences? Allow me to explain further by example.

The real-life scenario is that Ryan failed to ask his father's permission to borrow his torch to go caving. Ryan lost the torch and also failed to report that to his father. When Ryan's father needed the torch he asked Ryan if he had seen it and Ryan said 'no'. Some days later the friends that went caving with Ryan happened to mention to his father that they were sorry that the trip resulted in the loss of his torch. Instead of confronting Ryan about his dishonesty and lack of integrity, his father decided to tell him a metaphor when they were washing the car together the next weekend.

Ryan's father told a story about his friend at work whose son had borrowed his father's car and put a dent in the front fender. His son failed to tell him about the dent and the next day he discovered it and wanted to know how it had come about. The son said he didn't know how it got there and the father blamed his wife. Of course, his wife knew nothing of the dent and a heated discussion ensued. Finally, the son owned up and reported to his parents that he was driving too fast, jumped the kerb and scraped the car on a fence. In owning up to the lie, the son was saved the punishment of being grounded for a month and only had to pay for the repair of the dent. Not long after Ryan's dad had told him this story, Ryan owned up to losing the torch while caving and later lying about never having even seen the torch. His father hadn't had to play the bad guy because in this way Ryan had come to him with the news. Ryan was saved from a severe punishment and promised to replace his father's torch.

Small allegories can be made up on the spot and told as stories

to your children or you can spend some time composing them if you have the time. Each allegory needs to focus on one or two particular values and should highlight the consequences, good or bad, of using the value or not using the value. Let's look at some more examples.

Katie is five years old and her mother is teaching her about the value of unselfishness. The next day Katie and her mother are having visitors over and Katie's mother wants to see Katie be unselfish and share her toys with the other children. She has a choice. She can sit Katie down and give her a big lecture about sharing or she can make up a bedtime story that night about a girl called Cassie who never shared her toys with anyone and always ended up feeling sad because no one would play with her. One day a friend of Cassie's pointed out to her why the other children never wanted to play with her. It was because they thought she was selfish. Cassie ran home crying and sat on her bed in her bedroom thinking about what her friend had said. She came to realise that she had been selfish in not sharing things with her friends and the very next day she took her favourite doll over to her best friend and asked her if she'd like to play with it for a while. Slowly but surely, Cassie's friends realised that she was no longer selfish and Cassie discovered that it was twice the fun to share her toys with others.

Katie's mother told this story to Katie and surprise, surprise, the very next day there were absolutely no problems with Katie sharing her toys and her food with the visitors. As she tucked Katie into bed that night, Katie's mother smiled and told Katie that she was going to give her a special reward for being so unselfish and sharing all day with the visitors.

A similar method was used for Bradley aged 10 years. In Bradley's case, the lesson that his parents wanted to teach him was about honesty. At dinner one night, Bradley brought up the topic of honesty by saying that his friend at school always cheated on the weekly maths tests. Bradley's father told a story about a child that was in his class at school who always cheated and never seemed to get caught. It seemed so unfair to those who had to work hard and study for the test. Then one day this child was caught cheating and not only was he humiliated in front of everyone else in his school, he was suspended from school for one week which meant he had to catch up on a whole lot of work when he returned the following week. His parents grounded him for three months, which meant he was thrown off the cricket team because he couldn't go to the games or the practice sessions. His life was miserable all because he was dishonest. Bradley got the message. He realised that honesty was important and that when you are dishonest you sometimes suffer severe consequences. All that it took for him to learn this value was a short allegory that his father managed to make up on the spot.

Josie's mother had finally had enough of her untidiness and she desperately wanted to do something about it that would work. She had tried shouting, threatening, and grounding Josie, but none of these options worked. So she decided to take my advice and use a subtle allegory. One day when Josie was within earshot she began to tell Josie's sister about a magazine article that she had read about Josie's favourite rock star. Apparently this rock star's secret to success was having a clear mind at all times and the best way she found to do that was to have her house and, in particular, her bedroom all in order so that she knew where everything was. With everything in its place, she could focus on achieving her success. This allegory wasn't even delivered directly to Josie, but her mother made sure that she overheard the conversation. Sure enough, when her mother went up to Josie's room, two hours later she found Josie picking up her dirty clothes and rearranging her things. As Josie walked past her mother heading for the laundry room, she said something about a clear environment creates a clear mind and that that is the secret to success.

One of the most important things about teaching your children values is that you can't effectively teach anything that you're not willing to demonstrate yourself. It would be hypocritical to say 'do what I say, not what I do', and so it's up to you to practise what you preach. This places a lot of responsibility on you because guess who's going to pull you up when you don't demonstrate your values? That's right, your children. So you need to consider very carefully if teaching your children values is what you want to do. If you decide that it is, read on for some ideas on how to do just that.

Honesty and Integrity

Let's take our first value: honesty and integrity. Honesty is about being completely truthful and integrity is about being totally complete when you have been truthful. For example, if I told a lie then I would be dishonest. If I didn't tell a lie, but I didn't tell the whole truth because I left out some details, then I would be lacking in integrity.

Being completely honest with your children is an excellent way to demonstrate to them the true meaning of this value. Too many parents won't be honest with their children because they believe that they will have to wear 'a mood' later on from the child and so they take the easy way out and avoid the truth at all costs. One good guideline is to make sure that you don't let your children hear you telling little white lies either, especially on the phone. It's also a good idea to always follow through on any promises that you make, because this is a demonstration of honesty and integrity itself.

For very young children, a fun way to teach them about honesty and integrity is to play a game by looking through picture books. You ask the child to tell you if what you say is true or false. Point to a picture on the page and say, 'That is a dog'. If it is a dog the child will say 'true' and if it's not a dog she will say 'false'. You can also turn this game into a lucky dip game and replace the pictures with real objects or toys. With your eyes closed, you put your hand in and pull out a toy. You then tell the child what you think the toy is. She says true or false and then you open your eyes. This is a neat variation on the first game for those with toddlers and preschoolers.

Another fun game for the younger children is to draw a variety of faces with different expressions that communicate an emotion; that is, sad, happy, angry, funny faces. As your child looks at each face, ask her to tell you how that face feels and let her know that it's okay to be honest about feeling that way and telling Mum and Dad that she feels that way. I have found that this works very well because it prevents children from learning behaviours such as sulking (sadness or anger that is not clearly expressed) and shyness (fear that is not clearly expressed). Instead, they communicate clearly exactly how they feel.

A great game to play with school-aged children is a racetrack game. On paper or cardboard draw a racetrack, then divide the track into squares and mark the start and finish. On each square of the racetrack you write a scenario that deals with honesty or dishonesty or integrity and lack of integrity. Each child should have a toy car and a dice is thrown to show the number of squares the child should move at each turn. As your children land on a square they have to say if the scenario demonstrates honesty, dishonesty, integrity or lack of integrity. If you feel that integrity is too big a word to use with your youngsters then just stick with honesty. You can play a variation of this game with your older children by writing some scenarios that represent the two courses of action that the person could take — the honest and the dishonest. When your child lands on a square, she chooses a flash card with a certain scenario on it and she has to say which course of action she would take. You could then discuss with her both the short-term and long-term consequences of this decision.

It's usually about now that parents start to question the fact that they themselves haven't always been honest. They grapple with this for a while and then soon discover that even if they haven't always been honest they still want their children to have the benefit of this value and so they decide to go ahead and teach them as well as go ahead and try to be more honest themselves.

When it comes to teaching your older children about this value, it's very useful to discuss with them areas in your life where you currently have difficulty in being honest and in having integrity. Maybe also give them examples from your past where you were challenged by the lure of dishonesty or where you had a difficult choice to make about having a high level of integrity. This will make your children realise that they are not the only ones faced with these challenges as well as let them see that you are human, too. Discussing the different types of dishonesty is a useful thing to do with your older children. For example, discuss the difference between white lies, not telling everything, exaggeration and cheating. You could make up some scenarios that are examples of these four types of dishonesty and play a game where the children have to tell you which type of dishonesty belongs to each scenario.

Awards are a great idea for all of your children no matter what their age. When you all get together as a family you could present a small award to the child in the family who has demonstrated honesty and integrity. You could even give encouragement awards to those children who didn't quite make it but showed that they were making a concerted effort to demonstrate these values.

Of course with all of these values loads of encouragement are needed to spur your children on to demonstrating the values. You can't overencourage when it comes to learning these.

Integrity is all about keeping your word and sometimes we find it much easier to keep our word to others but we break our word to ourselves. For example, I find it easier to say yes to talking to a friend on the telephone even though I have made a promise to myself that on certain days I will devote all of my time to writing. A fantastic way of dealing with this tendency to break commitments to ourselves is to get each family member to write down (or you can write it for them) their integrity choices for the week; that is, what they are going to commit to doing this week. At the end of the week when you get together as a family, tally up the scores from each person as to whether or not they stuck to their intention, and get a percentage. See if you can aim for 100 per cent and if you don't make it the first week, aim for 100 per cent the second week. It's wonderful for parents to join in this as well. If you're the sort of parent who never does anything nice for yourself then make it one of your integrity choices to reward yourself in a particular way such as buying yourself flowers this week or having a massage.

Love

Love is one of my highest values and one that I constantly try to demonstrate to all children. A good way to start on the value of love is to ask each child about the different ways that someone can demonstrate love. This might be telling someone that they love them, doing something kind for them, looking after their hunger needs,

174

ironing their shirts or simply just being there for them in times of need. It's a great idea for parents to start letting their children know that all of the chores that they do for them is because they love them.

This is an easy way for parents to start verbalising that they love their children and also gives the children a new awareness that their parents are doing all of these things out of choice and love and that they could easily choose not to do them if they didn't want to.

A useful thing to do with all your children is to discuss the different types of love, such as love for a friend, love for a parent, love for a partner, love for a teacher and love for a family pet. This gives your children lots of information about the different types of love that we can feel and show. Discuss what is appropriate and inappropriate behaviour for each type of relationship. I'm sure that you'll be surprised by some of the comments that your children make about this. Sometimes we start out teaching and then we end up realising that our children are teaching us and that we're the ones doing the learning.

Unconditional love is what parents give to children. In adult relationships, however, there are conditions placed upon the individuals involved in the relationship. It's important to let children know the differences between the unconditional love that they get from their parents and the conditional love that exists in relationships. Otherwise they may go through their adult life searching for someone who will love them unconditionally and they may never find that someone.

I always believe that it's important to make it very clear to children when you don't like their behaviour that you still love them and that it's their behaviour that you don't like.

By providing small scenarios for your children about good and bad behaviour and then asking your children whether they think the parents loved the children or not, they can learn some distinctions between the behaviour and the love for the child.

For example, Danny wanted to ride his bike but it was raining. His mother said no, but Danny kept pleading and pleading until his mother got angry with him. Eventually Danny threw himself on the ground kicking and screaming. Do you think that Danny's mother still loves him? This can be played as a group game or can be used as a discussion at bedtime. You can use examples of brothers and sisters in the family to highlight the meaning of this to your children.

Service is the way that most parents show their love for their children, so why not encourage big brothers and sisters to show their love for their siblings by serving them. This can be as simple as helping a younger sister cut up her meat at dinner time. In turn, even the smallest child can show her love through service by carrying dirty dinner napkins from the table to the laundry room, helping Mum with putting flowers into a vase or some similar activity. It really doesn't matter how small the task is as long as it's done with love. Reading your young children stories about how people express their love through service and, of course, employing a valuable metaphor here and there, will go a long way towards teaching the value of love.

As a family you could choose a charity or some particular cause to devote some time and service to. This teaches your children to express their love through service to their community. They may want to sponsor a child from another country or sponsor a pet at the local zoo. They may clean out their closets and give all of their old clothes to a charity. This is a service to both their mother and the community at large.

If parents are not afraid to hug their children and show them affection no matter what their age then they are automatically showing their children how to express love through affection. Believe it or not, even teenagers love this, and it gives them that extra sense of security during those years when they need it the most.

Telling your children that you love them as they go off to school or as they go to sleep at night is a wonderful way of reinforcing the verbal expression of love. It's a bit like giving encouragement. When it comes to children you can never overencourage or say 'I love you' too much.

Parents are certainly challenged when their children reach late adolescence because then they ask a lot of questions about sex. Now is a good time to teach your children about the differences and similarities between sex and love, and how important it is to value sex as an expression of true love.

When it comes to the demonstration of love, use awards and rewards just as you did for the honesty and integrity values. Children love this.

Peace and Win–Win

Some successful parents I know use a set of stools set up in a certain area in their house to teach these values. When their children fight they have to go and sit on these stools until they sort out what their own responsibility was in starting the fight or in keeping it going. Another family that I know of use a 'talking pillow' that is shaped like a little heart. Whenever anyone has this pillow they get to talk and everyone else has to listen. That's the house rule. This family use it for serious discussions to ensure a win–win outcome and a peaceful discussion for all family members.

Peace is something that can encompass many qualities, such as calmness, patience and understanding. Discussing this with your children is a good entree into the area of peace and win–win values. Discuss what these words mean with each member in the family. Ask them what peace and win–win mean to them.

If you wish to have a peaceful environment to live in then ask your children how they think the family could create this. Some children I know actually suggested that their family always have peaceful music playing to soothe everyone's nerves and that a rule of no yelling should be instigated in their family. They did this and found that it worked brilliantly. They then instigated a rule where everyone takes their shoes off at the front door so that Mum has a clean floor and so they feel even more relaxed when they get home from school or work.

Having a warm bath is often a good way of relaxing and feeling peaceful. Standing in a line, tallest to shortest, and massaging the back and neck of the person in front of you is a fantastic way to relieve tension. Maybe this could be done before you all sit down for dinner. Whatever works for you and your family, use it.

The concept of win–win is often a complex one to explain to children, so once again the use of allegory may play an important role here. Play games where you give your children a problem and they have to find a win–win solution. For example, there are three lollipops and four children. Each of you wants a lollipop. What do you do? Try to choose situations from the very experience of your family to bring home the meaning with this game.

Maybe your children were fighting over lollipops or television shows just last week. Here's the opportunity to teach them a win–win way of handling it. Ask your older children how they would handle it. Often they come up with some very useful solutions that you would never have thought of yourself.

Discuss with your children the times when you were all clearly in a win–win situation and the advantages of that and also when you had the challenge of a win–lose situation and how you all handled that. This will give them a clearer picture of what it's all about and to see the win–lose method as a personal challenge. This will encourage them to take up that challenge instead of being a victim and saying 'They did it to me'.

One way of creating a peaceful household is to be peaceful and calm yourself, quite a challenge for busy parents of today. What can you do for yourself to put yourself into a peaceful, calm mood when you get home from work or when you've had a tough day at home? Think of solutions before the event so that when you start to feel uptight or angry you can take some other form of action to calm yourself down.

Have a peace award for the week or treat the peace award winner to a massage or a bath with pretty candles, bath oils and soft music.

As you can see, much can be done on your part to create the sort of peaceful household that you might wish for. Instead of complaining about the constant noise in the house, take some action and set up some rules, such as 'peace time'. This is when, for example, between certain times in the evening, everyone in the household is involved in some peaceful task or is encouraged to sit calmly and still. Peace time can be achieved with very little children by giving them a nap time or by reading them some of the visualisation stories from Chapter 6 of this book. Older children can sew, draw, paint or listen to calm soft music.

Teaching Commitment

Start by having a family brainstorm as to the meaning of commitment. What other words are the same or the opposite of the word 'commitment'? Discuss their meanings openly with the family.

Each family member could go through and outline the commitments that they have to themselves, their family, friends, to school and to their hobbies. Mum and Dad can point out to the younger children their commitments during this session. For example, the commitment to love their brothers and sisters and their mother and father, and the commitment to turn up at preschool and do the very best work that they possibly can.

Commitment is, by and large, doing what you say you will do. Ask each family member to give a 'hero story' example of when they lived up to a commitment. No matter how small and unimportant it may seem to them, a commitment to do something is an important value to learn.

With this value it's important that parents are seen to practise what they preach, and at the same time be flexible in giving their children second chances when they fall down on their commitments. Try to make it easy to catch them doing the right thing rather than punishing them when they do the wrong thing.

Asking your children their most important values here will give you an excellent idea of where they are prepared to put their commitment. The very young children can paint pictures on a poster of the things that they want to commit to. For example, one of their commitments might be setting the dinner table or feeding the family dog. They would therefore paint pictures on their poster of the dog and of the dining table. This can be hung up in their room to remind them of their long-term commitments. You can also do a weekly chart for short-term commitments. Older children can write their lists and put them up on their bedroom walls. Parents can write their lists and stick them on the refrigerator for everyone in the family to see.

With your teenagers you could have a discussion about your commitments to each other as husband and wife, father and mother. Discuss the finer distinctions of degree of commitment with your older children as this will have meaning for them. For example, one child may be very committed to baseball and have only a small commitment to geography. Teach them that our level of commitment affects our level of satisfaction. That is to say, 'we only get out of it what we put into it'.

Watch a video together as a family that highlights the value of commitment and loyalty. Discuss the video with your children afterwards to see what they thought of it and to see if they learned anything about commitment from it. Just by chance, you can often find good examples of loyalty and commitment in the daily shows your children watch on television. Even some cartoons highlight the importance of loyalty and commitment.

Of course, the use of bedtime stories and allegories can be invaluable for teaching these qualities.

Balance and Self-discipline

I'm sure you will agree with me that many of we adults could do with a refresher course on these particular values. I have a friend who suggested he buy me a seesaw to put outside my window to remind me to maintain a balance and prevent me from getting onto what I call the 'workaholic treadmill'. Maybe this is something that you need to look at yourself before trying to teach it to your children. Do you have a balance of work and play? Do you balance your time?

A good way of helping your child to see if she has a balance in her life is to get her to write a timetable of how she spends her time. In doing this, you can pinpoint any imbalance. Let's look at some examples.

Tony is eight years old and this is his timetable for the week:

MONDAY	TUESDAY	WEDNESDAY	THURSDAY
watch cartoons	watch cartoons	watch cartoons	feed the cat
feed the cat	get ready for school	get lunch order	watch cartoons
get ready for school	pack schoolbag	ready	have breakfast
pack schoolbag	have breakfast	have breakfast	pack bag for school
have breakfast	catch the bus	pack schoolbag	put out the garbage
catch bus	at school	catch the bus	catch the bus
at school	watch cartoons	at school	at school
soccer practice	scouts	soccer practice	watch television
homework	homework	dinner	do homework
reading practice	watch more	homework	watch television
dinner	television	watch television	have dinner
watch television	have dinner	reading practice	go to bed
go to bed	go to bed	go to bed	

FRIDAY	SATURDAY	SUNDAY
have breakfast	have breakfast	have breakfast
pack bag for school	get ready for soccer	get ready for church
watch videos	watch television	go to church
catch the bus	go to soccer with	play with friends
at school	Dad	have lunch
watch videos	have lunch	watch videos
have dinner	watch television	play with the
tee-ball practice	go to football with	computer
watch television	Dad	watch more videos
go to bed	watch television	have dinner
	have dinner	go to bed
	go to bed	

181

From looking at this schedule it seems that Tony has very little contact time with other children, or with his brothers and sisters, just to play. He spends most of his spare time watching television or doing sports. He doesn't have many chores around the house and he has virtually no time where he just relaxes and does nothing (this is apart from watching television and videos). His interests are quite limited and don't include anything that involves music, creative expression or general knowledge. There is no time set aside for family get-togethers because everyone in Tony's family eats at different times due to their busy schedules and on the weekends Tony is fairly busy playing soccer and football.

If we were to colour code Tony's schedule we may be able to see where it is out of balance. Let's colour code it as follows:

red = chores
dark blue = schoolwork or school-related
purple = sports or sports-related
yellow = music
dark green = art and creativity
brown = general knowledge
grey = television, videos or computers
orange = time with family
black = time with friends
white = religion
gold = meal breaks
silver = group activities
light blue = sleep time
light green = relaxing time to self

By counting up the number of times a colour appears, we get a clearer idea of how Tony spends most of his time. Overall, he spends most time getting ready for and attending school, and that is to be expected given the fact that there is quite a bit of preparation involved in getting ready and getting to and from school. When he is away from school the majority of his time is spent connected with television activities. If Tony were to cut down on some of this time it would leave him more time to spend with his family and friends and he may be able to get involved in listening to music, doing something creative or learning a little about general knowledge.

Of course there is much overlap on all of these events, but it does give you an idea of how to use the technique of creating balance in a timetable. Discuss with your children the advantages and disadvantages of having balance in their lives. What happens when they spend all of their time doing school work? What happens if all of their hobbies are ones that are done all alone? What happens if they never have any time on their own? Get them to draw up their timetables or you can draw them up for them and get them to colour code them to see where they need to cut back or add on. They can then negotiate with you for the add-on type activities of their choice.

Once again, the use of allegories will be valuable in pointing out the advantages and disadvantages of balance or lack of balance. Discuss with your children what they think self-discipline is. How does it relate to having a balance in life? Whose responsibility is it to initiate and maintain the self-discipline? What are some examples of self-discipline? Each family member could say what areas of their life they find it easy to be disciplined in and which areas they find it more difficult to have self-discipline in. You may want to brainstorm how each member of the family can help another member of the family to keep their self-discipline promises to themselves.

Teaching your children to write priority lists can help them achieve their goals in self-discipline. They can use their weekly integrity lists (see page 184) for this and prioritise the things that they need to do on that list for their self-discipline exercise. Prioritising can be done by writing down the list of things that need to be completed by the end of the week and then putting those things into one of these three categories:

- have to do (urgent)
- need to do (semi-urgent)
- want to do (not urgent but desirable)

Once they have categorised their items, they can then list the day and time that they commit to themselves to get these things done. Keep in mind that it's a good idea to have a balance, so that the 'have to' tasks get done, and some of both of the 'need to' and 'want to' tasks get done. The 'need to' tasks are things that aren't urgent but it would be good to get them done, whereas the 'want to' tasks are things that are special extras that make life more fun and more interesting. For example, Lucy's integrity list for this week is as follows:

Science assignment, letter to Nan, music practice, tidy my room, get hair cut, go to jazz ballet, wash Mum's car, do school homework, hire a video, help sister with project.

She categorised these items as follows:

HAVE TO: Do school homework, science assignment, wash Mum's car
NEED TO: Write letter to Nan, get hair cut, tidy room, help sister with project, music practice
WANT TO: Go to jazz ballet, hire a video

Lucy then assigned time slots in which to complete her tasks.

SCHOOL HOMEWORK: 6–9 pm every weeknight
SCIENCE ASSIGNMENT: 5–6 pm Monday and Wednesday, 4–6 pm Saturday and Sunday
WASH MUM'S CAR: 3.30–4.30 pm Friday
LETTER TO NAN: 6.30–7.30 pm Monday
HAIR CUT: 4–5 pm Thursday
TIDY ROOM: 9–10 am Saturday
MUSIC PRACTICE: 6–6.30 pm three nights per week
HELP SISTER WITH PROJECT: 6–6.30 pm Saturday and Sunday
JAZZ BALLET: 5.30–6.30 pm Thursday
HIRE VIDEO: 7–9 pm Friday

At the end of the week, Lucy had completed all of her 'have to' tasks as well as getting a hair cut, tidying her room and helping her sister with her project. She also managed to find the time to get to her jazz ballet class and to hire the video. She didn't get to write to Nan and so she put that as a 'have to' on her next week's integrity list of tasks to perform. She achieved a 90 per cent rating on achieving her integrity tasks and managed to do this with ease and a fair amount of fun. She found that by planning her tasks in this way she could do them so much more easily and fit in a lot more extra activities that weren't even on her list, such as a spontaneous invitation from friends to go shopping on Saturday.

Achieving self-discipline through the teenage years can sometimes be quite a challenge. However, if you sit down with your teenagers early on and make agreements as to what signs of self-discipline you would like to see them have for themselves then chances are they will adopt these when the time is right. Allowing them to discuss it with you and have their say can alleviate any desires to rebel, as you are treating them as true adults and respecting their contributions as much as you respect your own. This also assists them to make certain decisions in advance so that if a tempting opportunity arises to throw away the self-discipline and balance in life they have already made a commitment to be true to their agreement. This is an agreement not just to you their parents but ultimately the agreement is to themselves.

Courage

Courage is a very important value that can be taught early on to children. A good way to begin teaching it is to tell a bedtime story or an allegorical story about a child's show of courage. Make it one that will inspire your children and one that they can relate to. Perhaps it can be a mythical journey of a young boy who faces all odds to save a kingdom from destruction. Maybe you can use the movie *Star Wars* and the character of Luke Skywalker, or you could use the brave example of Princess Leia. Whatever you choose, make sure the story is full of excitement and challenges. When it comes to preschoolers learning to have courage, it's vital to reward even the slightest attempt at being able to ride a bike, play something on the piano or write their own name. Share with your children those times in your life where you really needed to draw on your inner strength and courage.

Ask them to share with you any memories that they have of their efforts to be courageous and applaud every one. Together with your children, compile a list of things that they believe would need courage to perform. For example, telling the truth, owning up to something that you've done wrong, being told that you are very sick and have to have an operation, losing someone that you love dearly. Also compile a list of actions that you and your children believe to be actions that show a lack of courage. For example, you could include running away when you've hurt someone, telling lies, letting someone else take the blame for something that you did, punching someone instead of discussing things with them, and not being honest with yourself.

Construct a board game where you give your children little scenarios. You can probably use some of the scenarios that you have written for some of the other values that you have worked on. Read the scenario out loud to the children and ask them to tell you what would be the courageous course of action to take and what action would demonstrate a lack of courage. Are there any actions in between?

Encourage your children to be adventurous. Provide for them situations where they may need to call upon their courage. This can be something as simple as trying new types of foods or doing physical activities that they've never tried before, such as climbing on monkey bars or climbing a tree. Allow them to write a list of things that they would need courage for and get them to list them in a hierarchy of easiest to hardest. Encourage them to work through the list over the next few weeks and put at least one of these items on

their integrity list for the week. Make sure that you reward them for each attempt to show bravery. This is necessary as it takes extra effort to demonstrate the value of courage.

One of the things that parents often forget to value is the incredible individuality of their children. Some parents, because of their own insecurities, worry about their children 'fitting in' and what other people might say. They feel more comfortable if their child is like everyone else. Surely children should be loved for their individual qualities? Look seriously at your own feelings about this. Do you want your children to fit in or do you want their individual talents to shine out.

Self-reliance and Independence

A useful way of beginning work on the value of self-reliance and independence is to ask your children to write a list of all of the things that they are good at. Ask them to list all of their talents, no matter how small. It may be that your two-year-old is particularly adept for her age at cleaning her teeth. That's a talent and something that should be included on her list. Maybe you could ask your children to write the lists on behalf of their brothers and sisters. This is a great

187

way of brothers and sisters realising how much their siblings care and admire them, even if they don't always show it. It is also useful to ask your children to write lists of the talents or habits that they are working on developing further.

Giving your children, no matter how small they are, the opportunity to make some of their own decisions about their lives gives them a true sense of the value of independence. This can be anything from setting their own rewards and punishments to allowing the youngest children to decide what they want to wear and what they want to eat that day. Try to be there for them to assist them if they need help but without forcing your help upon them.

It's vital that your children have a sense of taking responsibility for their own actions and not feeling that 'everyone is doing it to me' when something goes wrong. This will ensure that they develop into independent adults who take responsibility for their own lives. We already have enough professional victims in this world. Why not create the next generation into children who take responsibility for their lives. There are various ways that you can promote this idea. When your children have a disagreement, encourage them to own their part in the disagreement instead of just blaming the other child. Make a rule that they can't leave the house until they say what part they have played in the argument. Parents who do this with each other are constantly displaying a useful role model for their children as to how to solve conflict and take responsibility for your life. Whenever there is a household fight, encourage your children to 'be the solution, not the problem'. This gets them contributing their individual ideas and learning how to brainstorm solutions.

Another positive way of reinforcing this is to ask your children when they are in a competitive situation and don't win why they think that they didn't win. Encourage them to see that they are responsible for not winning without them feeling that they are to blame for not winning. This helps them in not blaming others or outside situations for their loss, as hard as such an attitude may be sometimes.

Encourage your children to help you with household duties and even your own hobbies. It takes a highly committed parent to allow their child to help them even when they know that it's going to make the task twice as long or that they may have to repeat it all over again later to fix some of the mistakes. Doing this will build your child's confidence in her ability to contribute her uniqueness to any situation.

When your children come up against things that they're not good at, remind them that the only thing standing in their way of being good at that particular skill is time and effort. Then remind them of the things that they are very good at already. How did they get to be good at those things? For many of these skills, the answer will be time and practice.

To encourage understanding of the value of self-reliance, it's a good idea to ask your children to make commitment lists which let them and everyone else know what they can count on *themselves* to perform. For example, your three- or four-year-old might say, 'I can count on myself to put my shoes on the right feet'. Your eight-year-old might say, 'I can count on myself to always tell the truth no matter what'. Your 15-year-old might say, 'I can count on myself to always look neat and clean all of the time'.

The commitments need to be ones that the children think of themselves and not necessarily things that you want them to commit to. They may need plenty of time to make their own decisions about this. As they may also need your assistance in thinking of things, be available for them, but don't dominate the situation. Introduce the concept of what you want them to do and when you're absolutely sure that they understand what they need to do, move off to another room and let them know you'll be there if they need any help. Of course it depends on the ages of your children whether or not you can disappear into the next room. The little children will probably need lots of guidance with this one.

Not doing your child's homework is another way of encouraging self-reliance and independence. Sometimes when a child is grizzling about her homework the easy way out is to do it for her and tell her the answers. In the long term, this is damaging for the child because she gets to learn that she can always be rescued by someone else. Soon she begins to expect it from others, and will have difficulty taking any sort of responsibility for herself.

Always praise your child's individuality and talents and any effort that she displays, no matter how small, to be independent and self-reliant. Once again, a reward at the end of the month or whatever time frame that you choose would be a useful way of reinforcing the use of this value.

Unselfishness

Many people feel that children, especially young children, are very self-centred, and that this is rightly so. I believe that even very young children can be taught the value of unselfishness. No matter what their age, children can often be far more in tune with others' feelings than we adults. How many times has your child sensed that you were upset without you having said a word about it? Children seem to have a natural instinct for picking these things up.

Talk with your children about what being unselfish means to them. What's the opposite of being unselfish and what are some examples of that? Let them tell you 'hero story' examples of times when they were unselfish. Tell stories of children who were unselfish and what the benefits of this action was to them in the long term. Similarly, tell them stories about children who were selfish and let them see what the consequences of that sort of behaviour is also. Tell your children your own 'hero stories' as well as some times when you were selfish and suffered the consequences of your behaviour.

With very little children, sharing can be a display of unselfishness. In a young child's life there can be many opportunities to share with others. Discuss with them how easy it is to share and how good it makes everyone feel, before they are in a situation where they need to be sharing with others. Then when the situation arises you can gently remind them of your discussion. Look back to the 'How to Compose an Allegory' section in this chapter and review how one parent used the technique of allegory to instil in her child the value of unselfish sharing.

By buddying-up your children for a week you can give them the task of supporting their buddy in as many ways as possible for that week. Maybe they will help their buddy make her bed or find pictures for a school project. Maybe they will help by making their buddy a special afternoon tea or breakfast on Sunday. Talk about how you and your partner are buddies and the different ways that you show that you love your partner by being unselfish and helping your partner out in a whole host of ways.

When it comes to making family decisions about where you will go out to on the weekends, it might be useful to let the children sort it out amongst themselves while you and your partner take special note of who is selfish and who is selfless. Reward the children who are selfless by letting them go to the place that they chose. Discuss with the other children why you have made that decision. It would also be useful to discuss that it's important to consider yourself as well as to be unselfish, and that it's not healthy to always be totally selfless and do the bidding of others. There is a fine line between meeting our own needs and meeting the needs of others.

Respect

Respect is a value that is often hard to describe to children because it is so abstract. Instead of trying to find a description, ask your children what examples they can think of of someone respecting someone else. You'll be surprised with what they come up with. Look at the different areas in your life where you show respect and discuss this with the children. Ask them to write a list of the different areas in their lives where they feel they should show respect to others. Respect for parents, teachers, coaches, friends, relatives. Respect for the environment that we live in.

What about respect for ourselves? How do we show this? By the way we keep ourselves neat and clean. By the way we stick to our commitments to ourselves. By the way we make promises to ourselves that we know we will keep. There are many opportunities in a child's day-to-day life for her to demonstrate respect for herself and for others. Therefore she has many chances at achieving the 'respect award' at the end of the month or the time period that you choose for this value to be demonstrated in.

One of the most valuable and most important ways that we show respect for ourselves is in the 'self-talk' we use on ourselves, that is to say, the language that we use inside our heads. Are we saying positive things that show respect for our talents and good points, or are we constantly showing little respect for ourselves by constantly putting ourselves down? Respect is also caring about how other people think and feel. Respecting other people's views is another important way that we show respect.

Play a game with your children where you read them a list of scenarios of children's behaviours and see if they think that the behaviours demonstrate respect or lack of it. For example, Gemma's mother asked Gemma to clean up her room as they were having visitors over that night and she wanted the house to look nice for them. Gemma waited until her mother was out of earshot and then she called her some very rude names. Is this showing respect or lack of respect?

In another example, Matthew was playing with a puzzle on the floor. Every time he got to a hard bit that he couldn't make fit he said, 'I'm so stupid'. Is that showing respect or lack of respect?

And lastly, Lucinda was playing with her sister's best doll with her sister's permission. When she got bored with the game, Lucinda just left the doll lying around. When her sister asked for the doll back, Lucinda found it outside with one arm torn off. The family dog had got to it because Lucinda had left it outside. Is this showing respect?

Kindness

Kindness is one of the most important values that we could ever teach our children. I see and hear stories every day from parents and children about how cruel some children can be. Even very small children can be thoughtless and unkind, and sometimes they are totally unaware that they are being unkind. The comments that many of them make and the behaviour that they use often do not reflect the value of kindness. So it's our job as parents to teach our own children how wonderful it is to be kind to other people and have them show you the same degree of kindness in return. Of course, this particular value really begins at home and so the best place to start is with brothers and sisters learning to be kind to one another.

Kindness is a combination of peaceability and courage. A simple act or word of kindness can have a profound effect on someone and so the use of this value should never be underestimated. Smiling a lot at home and showing your children that it's okay to smile at people whether you are walking down the street or buying something from a total stranger is a useful way to start teaching kindness. Ask your children to recount stories of times when their friends or teachers or brothers and sisters were particularly kind to them. Tell them your own stories from your life experience.

Brainstorm with the entire family what life might be like if there were no kind people in the world and everyone went around being very unfriendly. Discuss the differences between being shy and being unfriendly. Sometimes shy behaviour gets mistaken for unfriendliness. Discuss what sorts of behaviours you consider to be friendly, such as looking at someone when you talk to them, smiling at people, going up and introducing yourself to someone, helping someone carry something, offering emotional support through kind words when you think someone needs it.

The racetrack game, which makes use of scenarios of experiences that happen to children of differing ages, is also a very useful way of teaching kindness. Read the scenario out and ask the children if the response was a kind one or an unkind one. If it was unkind then ask them what would be a possible kind response. If it was kind, ask them what would be a possible unkind response. This will help even the youngest child make a clear distinction between the two types of behaviour.

The kind scenario might go something like this. Judy and Gill were playing in the backyard. Gill's mother called her inside to clean up her room. Instead of going home then and leaving her to clean up her room, Judy helped Gill clean up her room. It took half the time that it normally did and that left them more time to play. Was this an act of kindness or unkindness?

Give an award to the child in your family who introduced themselves to the most new people during the week. You could even start a star chart or lolly jar for this. Each child has her own chart or lolly jar. Whenever she introduces herself to someone new she gets to put a star on her chart or a lolly in her jar. The person with the most stars gets a prize and the person with the full lolly jar gets to decide who eats the lollies.

Teaching your own children to deal with the unkindness of other children is a fairly tricky thing to do. I always try to approach it by explaining that a child's teasing or unkind behaviour comes from insecurities or a home that maybe isn't much fun to live in. I always let the children know that they may not be able to change the other person's unkind behaviour, but they can certainly control the way they react or don't react to the unkind behaviour.

You can demonstrate kindness to your children by showing them the little kind things that you do for your partner, such as making breakfast in bed or sending flowers or giving them a good luck card or just a card to say you love them and appreciate them for being who they are. It's often the simple things that make all the difference.

With the very little children, craft activities can be useful in teaching them the differences between kind and unkind. They can make masks with kind faces and masks with unkind faces. They can then tell stories using the masks or make up little plays using the masks about being kind or unkind. You can use craft activities to make a flower or card that they can send to someone as a kind thought.

A great way of teaching kindness to brothers and sisters is to have a 'Be kind to ... day'. Each person in the family gets a turn to be the recipient of kind deeds from other family members for an entire day. This is great fun for both the giver and the receiver. You could even have a special prize for the 'Kindest Giver of the Day' and the 'Kindest Receiver of the Week'. This will teach the children that they can also show kindness in their receiving of good wishes and kind deeds from others.

Once again, make use of allegories by telling a story about your child's favourite role model. Highlighting that role model's extremely kind behaviour towards others will help teach the value and the positive consequences that lie in being friendly to others.

No matter which values you choose to teach your children, whether they be ones of courage, love, peace, honesty, balance, unselfishness, kindness or commitment, make sure that you always endeavour to be a role model yourself for these behaviours. Remember that from a very early age your children learn by imitating you. Always encourage them and try to catch them 'doing the right thing' rather than punishing them for doing the wrong thing. Share with them more of yourself by discussing times when you demonstrated or failed to demonstrate certain values. Most of all, learn to be accepting and flexible when they just don't quite meet the mark in demonstrating their use of the values that you teach them. Allow them to make mistakes and overencourage them every day.

Key Points

❖ Our values are the things we hold most dear. They are what motivates us and excites us.

❖ If we, as parents, fail to instil some important life values into our children, we run the risk of allowing them to develop without focus, maturity and independence.

❖ It is important to allow our children to develop their own values, as well as trying to teach them ours.

❖ One way of teaching values is to play games that are exciting, entertaining, and involve the children actively in learning about the concept of each value.

❖ Another way of teaching values is by the use of verbal allegories. Children love stories and allegory is an easy way of helping them understand positive and negative aspects of behaviour, without being too moralistic.

❖ Reward systems are essential in teaching values. They should be awarded on the basis of the child demonstrating by their behaviour that they understand and have incorporated a particular value into their life.

❖ Some of the values that I consider to be most useful to teach children are: honesty and integrity; balance and self-discipline; courage; peace and win–win; commitment; respect; kindness; self-reliance and independence; love; and unselfishness.

❖ Go easy and spend four or five weeks teaching one value to your children or pupils. You may prefer to leave it open-ended and see how long it takes them to develop and demonstrate their understanding of a particular value.

❖ In composing an allegory, it is a good idea to use role models that your children love, for example video characters or pop stars. Use characters that are similar in age and situation to your child.

❖ One of the most important things about teaching your children values is that you can't effectively teach anything that you are not willing to demonstrate in yourself. This places a lot of responsibility on you.

❖ No matter which value you are teaching your child, remember that from an early age your children learn by imitating your behaviour. Always endeavour to show you live your life by the values you are trying to instil.

CHAPTER NINE

Teaching Your Children How to Set Goals and Achieve Them

When parents start talking about goal setting with their children, they're often surprised to find that their children know a lot more about goal setting than they do. Such is the advantage of the education system in these times of strong orientation towards success. The truth is that there is a great deal more pressure on our children to achieve in a whole range of new areas, areas that perhaps weren't available to us as children. The result of this is that our children are put under a great deal of pressure to achieve. Why not give them every possible advantage by helping them to develop a system that will work in helping them achieve goals both at school and in sport, music, relationships — in fact, in any area of their lives in which they wish to achieve something? It's very simple, and it goes like this:

Step 1 Sit your child down at a time that is convenient and, using pen and paper, write down some areas of his life where he would like things to be different. For example, a young child may choose schoolwork, sport and friends, and a teenager may choose sport, social life and career preparation.

    For our purposes, write these three categories down on the

paper as headings. Now choose the first area that you want to set goals in and ask the child to think of a sentence that is both positive and in the past tense — that is, as though it has already happened. For example, Lucy decided that she wanted to work on the area of schoolwork. Her goal statement was this: 'I, Lucy, have improved my spelling quota by three points. I now find spelling more enjoyable and easier to do.' The first part of this statement is in the past tense and it is positive.

Lucy needed help to form this statement so you may find that you need to help your child to do this, particularly in the beginning. After a while, he'll be an old hand at forming goal statements and he'll be able to help you with your goals. Once you have this statement and you've checked to see that it is in the past and it is positive, then go on to the second step.

Step 2 The second step involves asking your child whether he can start the goal all on his own and maintain it on his own. That is to say, is the goal self-initiated and self-maintained? If we look at Lucy's goal, we can see that it will be up to Lucy to do the work necessary to move her quota up three points and keep it there. She is responsible for finding spelling more enjoyable and easier. No one can do this for her, although you or a tutor could help her along the way. Ultimately, the goal that your child sets has to depend on him to make it happen. He can't rely on the efforts of anyone else, although extra support may be beneficial. Once this has been established, you can move ahead.

Step 3 In the next step the child is asked to be what I call 'sensory specific'. Ask your child to think specifically about how he will look once he has achieved his goal. Will he look happy or sad? Will he look more relaxed? Get him to make a picture up in his head of how he will look once he has achieved his goal. He can have other people in his picture, too. How are these people acting towards him? Is it very different from how they would usually act? Children are usually very good at doing this if you set it up as a fun game in the first place and not a highly serious task that has to be done.

Once he has his picture and it's exactly as he wants it, ask him to turn it into a moving picture like the television (if he hasn't already). Ask him to listen very closely and see if he can hear himself talking in the picture. What is he saying about himself? Are there other people in his picture who are talking about him? Lucy had a picture of herself in the classroom. She was smiling broadly as she heard the teacher tell the class that she had gone up three points on her spelling quota. Then Lucy heard herself say 'I did it' in a really excited voice. By making up a picture and adding the sound to it, you are forming an identity in your brain of someone who has already achieved your goal.

Now ask your child how he thinks he might feel when he achieves this goal. Will his body feel relaxed? Will he tingle all over? Will he feel cold or warm? Where exactly does he feel this feeling? Lucy said that she felt a tingling feeling in her tummy and it moved around. It was a very warm feeling and very nice to experience. If you find that your child can't find a feeling or can't put sound to his picture then let him stay with what he has. With practice, he will be able to make up the pictures, sounds and feelings very quickly and easily.

Step 4 This step is a crucial one. This is where we set the evidence procedure that will let us know that we have achieved our goal. Lucy's evidence was that she would go up three quota points in spelling. It is essential that the evidence procedure that you and your child use is measurable and specific. It wouldn't be useful for Lucy to have just said, 'My spelling has now improved and I enjoy it more', because how do we measure the improvement? The evidence procedure needs, therefore, to involve some numbers or some form of measurement within it. Lucy could have also included in her measurement that as well as going up three quota points she would look more happy and she would have that warm comfortable tingling feeling in her tummy every time she thinks of or does some spelling work. This would make her results even easier to establish by adding the feeling dimension to it. This will also encourage Lucy to become more independent because no one can know how she feels except for herself. That is to say, she would have to be the one to say whether or not she had in fact achieved that feeling part of her goal. Lucy could also include in her evidence procedure a time frame for when she will have achieved this goal — for example, she might want to increase her spelling quota by three points by the end of the school term.

Step 5 This step is sometimes a tricky one, but with practice it will become second nature to you. In this step you are finding out from your child what the bottom-line reason is for him wanting whatever it is that he's set for his goal. You do this by asking him why he wants it. When he answers ask him why he wants that. Keep asking him, 'Why do you want that?' until you get to what seems to be the bottom-line reason. For example, Lucy said she wanted to improve her spelling so that she'd come in the first three in the class. Why did she want to come in the first three in the class? She wanted to impress her teacher. Why did she want to impress her teacher? Her teacher would really like her and then the other kids would like her. Why did she want the other kids and her teacher to like her? Then she would feel like she fits in, that she belongs. This was Lucy's bottom-line reason for wanting to improve her schoolwork, and in particular, her spelling skills. This is called the 'reasoner'. It is the bigger reason that we have for wanting what we want.

For many children, the bottom line is that they want to belong, be accepted or want to be loved. In fact, when we do our own goal-setting strategies as adults and work out our own bottom-line reasons, we often find similar reasons exist for our goals as those of our children. We all just want to be accepted for who we are, feel as though we belong and to be loved. That's a good reason, isn't it?

When someone hits their bottom-line reason for wanting something, if you are very observant you will probably notice some change in their physiology such as a change in their posture, facial expression, hand movements, voice and even the way they breathe. Most of us can just tell when someone has reached the bottom line and it's usually done by observing these subtle changes in the other person.

Step 6 This step is what I call the 'whole-person check'. This means that you need to check with your child if this new goal is going to be suitable in every aspect of his life. For example, if your teenager wants to greatly enhance his social life because he is somewhat shy, if he does this and starts going out with friends every night, what will happen to his schoolwork? If your child wants to become more assertive at school, will this be a useful goal to have in the setting of the family? You can do a whole-person check by asking your child to close his eyes and pretend that he already has his goal. Now ask him to see himself in the playground, in the classroom, at the dining-room table and at soccer practice. Get him to check all of these situations to see if he still wants the goal in all of these settings.

This step is probably the most important step of all. If we don't do a whole-person check then the child's brain will prevent him from achieving his goal because there will be a part of him deep down that really doesn't want it to come true. So we need to consciously look at all of these areas. Sometimes you will find that when you do this your child realises that he really didn't want what he first set out to have and he will change his goal statement accordingly. Never forget to do this step if you truly want to achieve that goal.

Step 7 Now look at the different contexts that your child would like to have this particular goal in. Maybe he wants to have this goal only at school and not at home, or maybe he wants the goal to be present only in his social life. Ask your child which situations he thinks that the goal would be useful to him in.

Step 8 The second last step in this process is also a very crucial one: the creation of a future memory — a memory of the outcome that your child wants but a memory that is placed in the future. In other words, you ask your child to imagine himself in three different contexts, three different situations where he has the outcome. He must imagine himself in this situation as though it were a movie. The events and the picture that occur must be exactly how the child wants things to be and it must include him having his outcome. Ask him to make his picture in colour if he can, and also add sound to the picture. Once the picture and the sound are to the child's liking, ask him to place himself in the picture. Ask him to actually step into the picture and experience what it feels like to have his outcome — that is to say, have his goal already achieved. Once he has fully experienced the feeling, ask him to step back out of the picture. This will trick his brain into knowing that his outcome is possible and will encourage him to both consciously and unconsciously go out and achieve his goal.

Step 9 The final step is to determine what the first step will be in achieving the goal. For Lucy and her improved spelling goal it might be to do an extra 10 minutes of spelling homework each night.

In this way, you have set up the strategies for your child to achieve his goal. Now it's up to him to go out and get it.

Simple really, isn't it?

Now let's look at some scenarios of children's goal-setting strategies.

Example Scenarios

Henry wanted to have more friends at school so he wrote his goal statement as follows: 'I, Henry, have made a group of good friends to hang out with on the weekends.' This has been stated positively and is in the past tense. It is self-initiated because it is up to Henry to find these new friends and keep them as friends. In Henry's colourful moving picture of himself he was surrounded by a group of five new friends. He added sound to this and noticed that they were all laughing and having a good time and they were all really listening to what Henry had to say. Henry stepped into his movie and found that not only did he look really happy, but he felt very alive and full of energy in this situation. He was saying to himself, 'Wow, I really can be popular. Look at all of my friends.'

Henry's evidence procedure stated that in three months' time he would have five friends that he could choose to hang out with on the weekends. These friends had to like him and accept him. The evidence procedure for this is that they would really listen to what Henry had to say. When Henry was asked what the reason was for him wanting to have these new friends to hang out with, he said that it was to be popular. When asked why he wanted to be popular, he said that he wanted to be liked. When asked why he wanted to be liked, he said that he wanted to be liked so that he would have people around him. When asked why he wanted to have friends around him, he said that he didn't want to be lonely any more. This was Henry's bottom line and his father could tell that by the fact that Henry's posture changed (he dropped his eyes down to the ground) and his breathing changed (he took in a sharp breath before saying this).

Then Henry's father did a whole-person check with Henry to see if it would be okay for him to have these friends around all of the time, and Henry said that it wouldn't but that's why he'd said he wanted to hang out with them on the weekend. Henry's father clarified with him the different contexts that he might want these friends to be around in, and Henry decided that maybe he would also like these friends to be around at lunchtime at school also. Henry then altered his goal statement as a result of this to read: 'I, Henry, have made a group of friends to hang out with on the weekends and during lunchtime at school.'

Henry's future memory task consisted of a picture of him at lunchtime at school surrounded by his friends, having lots of fun and laughing. He also had a picture of going to the movies and rollerblading with these friends on the weekend.

When Henry was asked what his first step would be in finding these friends, Henry decided that maybe he could find them by joining the school drama group or by trying out for the athletics team. Henry's father thought that that was a great first step. Henry did this and found that, sure enough, within three months he was surrounded by a large group of friends that he could mix with both at school and on the weekends. In fact, Henry was the happiest his father had seen him in a long time.

Margie was four years old and she wanted to have more time with her mother. Her mother helped her to plan her goal statement. Together they came up with this: 'I, Margie have had an extra 30 minutes with Mummy on her own each week.' Margie made up a picture and it consisted of her and Mummy sitting in her bedroom talking and playing with her dolls. Her and Mummy were chatting in friendly voices and she felt really good inside. Although Margie's statement was stated positively and is in the past, it wasn't necessarily self-initiated and self-maintained because it would depend on her mother having the time to spend with her. Margie's mother decided that half an hour over seven days was only about five minutes per day and that she could certainly handle that, so they went ahead with

Margie's goal statement. Margie's evidence procedure was that Mummy would actually set the time aside to spend with her, and her reasoner was that she wanted to be loved. When the whole-person check was done, it seemed that all of Margie was happy to have the extra time with Mummy, even if it was at a time when her favourite television program may be on. The contextualising of this meant that the extra time was set for the context of home only. The future memory of this was the same as Margie's initial picture, and she could easily see herself in the picture with her Mummy and then step out of the picture.

The first step to achieving this goal was that Margie would have to remind her mother before dinner every night that they needed to have their five minutes after dinner together. This worked out so well for Margie and her mother that they decided to do the same thing with Margie's big brother Steve. Even though the five minutes went pretty quickly, it was the fact that Mummy was happy to spend the five minutes just with Margie alone that made the difference to her. She felt special and loved. So did Steve.

John's goal was to find a girlfriend that he could really relate to. John's father really enjoyed helping him with this goal as it made him feel very young again what with all of this talk about girlfriends. Together they came up with this goal statement: 'I, John, have found a fantastic girlfriend who really suits my personality and who is great fun to be around.'

John felt that he could go out and find such a girl and once he found her he could maintain the relationship, so his goal was positively stated, in the past tense and self-initiated and maintained.

It was pretty easy for him to form a picture of himself with this girl who suited him and was fun to be around. So he made the picture colourful and added in his favourite song in the background as well as lots of laughter. He could feel really relaxed in his body and he was bright and full of energy and enthusiasm. Therefore, John established the sensory specifics of his goal.

John then had to set an evidence procedure and he decided that the evidence would be that he felt relaxed, full of energy and knew that he was having a great time with this girl. He put a time frame of two months in which to find this new girlfriend.

When John's father tried to find out what John's reasoner was, John said that he wanted a girlfriend so that he would have someone special to care about who would also care about him. John's Dad could see from John's body position and voice tone that he was very clear about this and that it in fact was his bottom-line reason, so they had to search no further.

When John and his father did the whole-person check, John decided that it would be okay for him to have this relationship with the new girlfriend as long as he was able to keep some balance between the relationship and his schoolwork and his sporting activities. John felt that he could work the relationship into his sporting activities, but that he would need to contextualise it to after homework and assignments were done, on the weekends and at sporting events. So John and his father put in these safety checks to make sure that John would achieve his balanced lifestyle.

It was easy for John to then go ahead and make up pictures of himself with his new girlfriend at sporting events, out on the weekend, and talking on the phone after he'd completed his homework. Each picture was in full colour and he could add music and the sound of his own voice quite easily. He could even include the sound of his own laugh. He felt alive and happy and full of energy and excitement in each situation's picture. The only thing remaining to do was to work out what the first step was to finding this girlfriend.

John's father asked John whether there were any girls at school or at youth group that he liked and felt relaxed around. John could pinpoint exactly who this girl was and all he needed to do was to go ahead and ask her out. Easy. It looked like John would have his relationship much faster than he thought. It was also very useful that his father reminded him that if this girl said no then it just meant that she wasn't the right one and that he should just go ahead and ask someone else. So John was all set to go out and achieve his goal thanks to the help of his father using this goal-setting system.

Trish wanted to know how she could be more relaxed during her exams and achieve better results because of this. Her mother suggested that maybe she should read to Trish or make a tape for her of some guided relaxation exercises, and so they decided to set up a goal around that. They already had their first step, that is to say, they would use the resources available to them to achieve their outcome. Trish decided on the statement 'I, Trish, have performed better by using relaxation techniques to calm me down in both school and piano exams and in sports tryouts.' Well, it seemed that Trish had already partly contextualised her goal. This goal was positive and in the past tense as well as self-initiated and maintained, even though Trish was enlisting her mother's assistance in making the relaxation tapes for her.

When Trish was specific about this goal and made up her movie in her head, she saw herself sitting in her maths exam, very relaxed and confident. She felt different from how she normally felt in exams. In her picture, she felt very relaxed in her body and her mind was devoid of the panicky thoughts that she usually experienced in this situation. Trish decided that her evidence procedure should be that she would feel this way in her next lot of exams for both maths (her most difficult subject) and in her piano exam. The results of both of these exams should reflect her change in attitude.

Trish's mother asked her why she wanted to be more relaxed and perform better at her schoolwork and the answer was that she wanted to be a success. Why did she want to be a success? So that she would be loved. Simple really.

When the whole-person check was done on this particular goal, it seemed that there was no part of Trish that was in opposition to this new, relaxed and more successful Trish emerging. Trish decided that she would be happy for this outcome to occur for all subjects and extracurricular activities, but in particular, for piano lessons and for mathematics.

When she put her future pictures into action, Trish saw herself, in both the maths exam and piano exam, doing brilliantly on the test material and looking and feeling very relaxed. She then needed to get on to her first step, which was to listen to the relaxation tapes every morning before going off to school and every evening before going to sleep. Trish did this and found that the results she achieved were markedly improved on her previous term's results. Furthermore, her piano teacher noticed how much more relaxed Trish was in general, and her technique improved overall.

Once you have helped your child to find the area in which he wants to reach a goal and you have helped him to write the goal, it's often a good idea to draw a flow chart to represent the different steps and time frames that he will need to complete in order to achieve his long-term goal. Below are some examples of flow charts to suit the scenarios already presented.

Lucy's Goal

'I, Lucy, have improved my spelling quota by three points. I now find spelling more enjoyable and easier to do.'
Evidence procedure: To increase spelling quota by three points by the end of term.

Step 1: Spend 10 minutes extra on spelling homework from week one to week three. Have tutoring in spelling once per week with Mrs Davey. (Aim: To increase spelling quota by one point by week three of term.)

Step 2: Spend 15 minutes extra on spelling homework for weeks four to seven. Continue tutoring with Mrs Davey once per week. (Aim: To increase spelling quota by one more point by week seven of term.)

Step 3: Spend 15 minutes extra on spelling homework for weeks eight to ten.

Continue tutoring with Mrs Davey or enlist Mum's and Dad's help with extra work. (Aim: To increase spelling quota by a third point by week ten of term.)

Step 4: Celebrate by going out to McDonald's for lunch on Sunday with my friends.

Henry's Goal

'I, Henry, have made a good group of friends to hang out with on the weekends and during lunchtime at school.'

Step 1: Join the school drama club and make friends. Take one month to do this.

Step 2: Have a barbecue on the weekend and invite the friends from drama group over. Do this in week four. Ask Mum and Dad for help with this step.

Step 3: Go up to some of these friends and spend time with them during the lunchbreak.

Step 4: Offer to help some of these friends to learn their lines for the play. Do this in week five if appropriate.

Step 5: Invite all of these drama friends to go rollerblading on the weekend. Understand that not all of them may want to go with me.

Step 6: Join the local athletics club. Go out of my way to talk to some of the kids there. Do this by week six.

Step 7: Invite some of the athletics people and some of the drama group to go to a movie on the weekend. Do this by week seven.

Step 8: Look around and see how many friends I have to hang out with during lunchtime at school and on the weekends.

Margie's Goal

'I, Margie, have had an extra 30 minutes with Mummy on her own each week.'

Step 1: Remind Mummy that she needs to spare five minutes after dinner. Get out the game that I want to play with Mummy and have it ready in my room.

Step 2: Continue to remind Mummy each night about the five minutes. Be ready to spend the five minutes whenever it suits Mummy to give the extra time.

John's Goal

'I, John, have found a fantastic girlfriend who really suits my personality and who is great fun to be around.'

Step 1: Ask the girl that I like at youth group out on a date by the end of next month.

Step 2: Notice how I feel when I'm with her and see if I'm relaxed and full of energy like my picture says I want to be.

Step 3: If I don't feel this way around her then ask someone else that I like to go out with me and try again by the end of six weeks.

Trish's Goal

'I, Trish, have performed better by using relaxation techniques to calm me down in both school and piano exams and in sports tryouts.'

Step 1: Ask Mum to make up the relaxation tapes for me.

Step 2: Listen to the relaxation tapes every morning before going to school and every evening before going to sleep. I do this every day leading up to my maths exam and my piano exam.

Step 3: When I am in piano classes and maths classes I will remember how relaxed I felt when listening to the tapes.

So you can see how easy it is to help your child write simple goals and the steps to achieve them.

Planning Schedules

One of the most difficult tasks that we are all faced with today is the challenge of finding a balance between the different areas of our lives. In my business I have been exposed to many different ideas of how to organise time effectively and efficiently. It struck me that if fathers were using some sort of time plan in their work and mothers were keeping a diary for their important appointments, why shouldn't children have some sort of visual way of planning out their own schedule? Not only could this be a highly useful thing to do, but it could be made into a really fun craft activity. Let's explore this further.

Ask your child to tell you or to write down for himself all of the different things that he does in each day. For example, here is Tom's daily schedule for a typical week. Tom is eight years old.

MONDAY	TUESDAY	WEDNESDAY	THURSDAY
Get dressed	Get dressed	Get dressed	Make bed
Make bed	Make bed	Make bed	Have breakfast
Have breakfast	Have breakfast	Have breakfast	Get dressed
Pack schoolbag	Pack schoolbag	Pack schoolbag	Pack schoolbag
Violin practice	Watch cartoons	Feed fish	Talk to Grandma on
Go to school	Go to school	Go to school	the phone
Swimming training	Do homework	Do homework	Go to school
Dinner	Watch TV	Play with friends	Swimming training
Homework	Dinner	Have dinner	Have dinner
Reading	Reading	Watch TV	Watch TV
Watch TV	Go to bed	Do reading	Do homework
Go to bed		Go to bed	Do reading
			Go to bed

FRIDAY	SATURDAY	SUNDAY
Watch cartoons	Have breakfast	Watch cartoons
Get dressed	Get into uniform	Have breakfast
Make bed	Go to soccer	Go to church
Get lunch order	Lunch with team	Have lunch
ready	Watch TV	Talk to Grandpa on
Go to school	Violin practice	the phone
Violin practice	Have dinner	Watch TV
Do homework	Wipe up dishes	Help Dad wash the
Watch TV	Set the table for	cars
Reading	breakfast	Set the table for
Go to bed	Watch TV	dinner
		Have dinner
		Go to bed

It seems from looking at Tom's schedule that he doesn't have a lot of contact with other children planned into his schedule, although he does seem to watch a lot of television. He has a lot of chores and practice sessions for violin and swimming training, but he doesn't have much time to himself other than when he watches television. He doesn't have many activities in his schedule that the family do together.

By looking at your child's schedule you can see in what areas he is overloaded and what areas need to be built up and given more of a priority. My suggestion would be that Tom should watch less television but be given more time to himself to do whatever else he wants, such as reading a book, building a model, talking more with his grandparents on the phone, maybe seeing more of them. These decisions should be made by both of you. Maybe looking at your child's schedule will highlight for you how much time you *don't* have together as a family. Maybe that's something that your child would like more of. Maybe he wants more time with his grandparents or maybe he wants to go on more outings so he can explore other activities outside the home. Of course, this all has to fit into the family's schedule as a whole but you can see that just by looking at one of your children's weekly schedules it highlights what you are doing as a family.

One great idea is to record all this information on a large piece of butcher's paper and put it up on the wall. Then colour code different areas of your child's day and colour these in on your child's schedule (see example on page 213). Then you can see whether or not there's a balance or where things are out of balance. For example, let's say you colour chores in red, schoolwork in blue, family activities in green and play activities in orange. Once you've done this you can alter the schedule more easily to achieve that much sought-after balance. Most children find making up their timetable terrific fun, apart from the fact that they are getting special time alone with you to look at their schedule and draw up their chart. You can make this even more fun by letting them colour-in their chart and maybe colour a border around the chart or draw pictures to represent the different activities. Maybe you would like to do a colour-coded chart for your own life schedule and see for yourself where things may be out of balance.

Key Points

❖ Goal setting is a very valuable activity for both yourself and your children.

❖ The steps used in the goal-setting procedure can be remembered by the use of the mnemonic + S S E R W C F. 'Plus sentences seem to end in really wonderful catchy fun.'

  + — State the goal in the positive and make it in the past tense.

  S — The outcome must be about your child. He must be responsible for initiating the steps leading to the outcome and maintaining them. That is, he has to be able to start the steps leading to his outcome and keep them going himself.

  S — The outcome must be sensory specific. Your child should make up a moving picture of his outcome and then add sound, voices and feelings to it. State exactly how he will be looking, acting, talking and feeling once he's achieved his outcome.

  E — This is the evidence procedure. What is going to be the evidence that will let your child know that he has achieved his outcome?

  R — This is the bottom-line reason behind why your child wants his outcome. This can be discovered by repeatedly asking him why he wants to have whatever it is he wants until you reach the point where you know he has reached his bottom-line reason.

  W — This is the whole-person check. You ask your child whether he would be happy having his outcome in every area of his life. Check this in as many contexts as you can think of — school, with friends, with grandparents, with teachers, with brothers and sisters.

C — This is where you choose specific contexts in which your child wants his outcome to occur.

F — This is the future memory that you place into your child's mind so as to get his brain working towards his outcome. Get him to do this by picturing clearly in his chosen contexts a picture that is colourful and has sound and voices (if possible) and is absolutely the way he wants things to be. When he has that picture, ask him to step into the picture and see what it feels like to already have what he wants. How does it make him feel and where in his body does he feel that feeling?

❖ It is vital that you plan the first step that your child needs to take in order to have whatever he wants.

❖ You can do a flow chart that represents all of the steps that your child needs to do to get to his goal.

❖ By drawing up a timetable of how your child spends his time each day and then colour coding it according to the different areas of his life, you can see where his activities may be out of balance and adjust his timetable accordingly.

CHAPTER TEN

Activities to Stimulate Communication and Self-expression

Having children can be a wonderful opportunity for you as parents to relive all of the fun aspects of your childhood, all of the play and activity that goes with being a child. Joining in activities with your child where you yourself return to a childlike state of fun will build incredible rapport between you. It reduces the differences between the two of you and draws you closer together for a more intimate relationship. Furthermore, it teaches your child that you are also human and that you can have fun.

All the games and activities set out below also function on another level. As well as providing fun and an opportunity to build rapport, they offer the child many opportunities to express herself fully through both verbal and non-verbal communication. Some of the activities provide an opportunity to resolve inner conflicts that the child may have about her self-image and about the issue of parental control. Family conflict and misfortune can be explored by using some of the activities. I have used all of these activities with children and they love them.

The activities don't take very long to perform, so you could easily schedule one or two a week as a way for you to spend special individual time with your child. When you read through the activities you may think that they would only be suitable for very young children, but you will be surprised to discover how much your older children will enjoy revisiting the days of fun and craft and play. Why not give it a go!

Storytelling

In this game everyone takes turns in making up a story by painting or drawing pictures on a large piece of paper. Each person adds to the story as they draw their contribution to the picture. You can help your child to draw pictures that she wants to include but are too difficult for her to draw. The advantage of this game is that you don't have to have any real skill at painting or drawing to participate and have fun. This game works on building sound communication skills as it stimulates your child's language development. Once she has expressed herself non-verbally by painting or drawing, she can tell the story that the pictures represent.

Fairytale Murals

For this activity you need a long sheet of paper or a number of sheets stuck together and, preferably, stuck up on a wall. Each person draws their fairytale in a sequence of drawings that move through time. At the end, each person reads their story out to the rest of the family group. This particular activity stimulates the imagination and verbal skills of each child. It also teaches essential knowledge of the sequencing of events and the use of past, present and future tenses.

Mask Making

Making masks is great fun as a craft activity and also as a means of stimulating language and self-esteem. You and your child draw a mask that represents a side of yourself that you don't like. You can use virtually any materials you find around the house. The mask can be made on a paper or plastic plate and you can paint the face, draw it, or make it three-dimensional with papier-mâché. Once the mask is completed, you can use it for discussion and role play. You can talk about the different characters that your masks represent. From my experience, this usually ends up in everyone rolling on the floor having fun. It's also a way of accepting the shadow or unacceptable parts of ourselves as being just that, parts of ourselves. It doesn't make these parts wrong or right, but it means that we accept who we are and the different aspects of us that make up our personality. This allows the more negative emotions such as fear, anger or jealousy into the realm of normality and acceptability.

Who's Got a Secret?

In this game, each family member draws a secret without telling the others what their secret is. It's a good idea to discuss what having a secret means so that your child understands the concept of a secret. Swap your drawings with another person and let them try to guess what your secret is. The game involves the powers of deduction and imagination and focuses attention on the meaning of secrets. Secrets can be an issue for any group of people whether it concerns the telling of them or the keeping of them.

Add-on Paintings

For this game it's best to have a very large sheet of paper. Start by drawing the head of a person or an animal and then fold the paper over to cover up the head and then pass it on to the next person. The next person draws the neck and then folds over the paper and passes it on to the next person. You continue as a group to draw the rest of the animal or the person and then you open up the paper and see

how unusual your animal or person looks. You can use this exercise to paint pictures of objects or to make up pictures of monsters. It's lots of fun. This activity involves teamwork and an appreciation of the way animals or people may be different from what is considered 'normal', but can be beautiful nevertheless.

Life-sized Dolls

Ask someone to lie down on a large piece of paper (or on pieces of paper stuck together) on the floor. With a pen, draw around them so that you have traced an outline of their body. Using paints, material, wool and any other materials that you can find, fill in the rest of the person. Discuss the results. The discussion helps deal with the issues of self-image and can be used to look at how we change physically as we grow up. You can do this by comparing the life-sized dolls of the children at different ages.

Present Time

Each person paints a present that they would like to give each other person in the group. They then cut it out (with help if needed) and give it to the person they have drawn it for to take with them and keep, just like a real present. This highlights the concept of giving and receiving. It is particularly useful when trying to teach the value of unselfishness.

Family House Collage

Using pictures from magazines and any other objects, such as material, wool, old egg cartons, milk cartons, cotton reels, and plastic, make a collage of the house that you would love to live in. Discuss the collage when it is finished and compare the good things and the bad things about this perfect house with your current house or flat. It is likely that everyone will have different ideas and the discussion can be useful in highlighting the value of peace and win–win if you make it a rule that every family member has to agree what goes into the perfect house. This activity also encourages everyone to think about what aspects of their environment they value. It can also be used to show your children how to weigh up pros and cons.

Bossy Boots Game

In this game the parent has to paint a picture that is fully directed by the child. The child is boss and has to tell the parent what she can use, when she can use it and exactly what has to be done. This is a good role-reversal game and gives the child an experience of having total control in a situation that is non-threatening for the parent. This game also teaches the child to give accurate instructions to another individual. For parents who usually parent by control, the activity provides an opportunity to let go of their role easily and in a fun, non-threatening situation. It can be as rewarding for them as it is for the child. However, you should reverse the roles at the end of the game to make sure your child returns to being the child and you have your role of parenting returned to you.

Play Dough Families

In this game each participant makes dolls with play dough that represent each family member. Once the dolls are made, you can make them perform a little role play about an actual event in your family life or an imaginary one. The game can be used to explore the children's 'ideal day with the family', or to resolve and discuss any misfortune that may have occurred. For example, if a child has been caught stealing money at some time, you could address the situation through the game rather than confronting them directly. You could even replay the scenario so that it ends in a preferable way, with the child deciding to return the money on her own. This is a very versatile game and can be used to emphasise any of the values that you may want to teach from Chapter 8.

Favourite Things

Each family member draws or paints a picture of the things that are most important to her in the house where she lives. This may be a family pet or a teddy bear, or a favourite book or video tape. This exercise helps individuals clarify what possessions they value most and allows them to see that it is perfectly acceptable for each person to have different values.

Childhood Memories

In this game, both the parents and the children draw a picture and tell a story about an event that happened to them when they were very little. This is great fun for the children because they get to hear stories about when Mummy and Daddy were little children. I find that children are always fascinated by this activity. It is important to note that the memory doesn't necessarily have to be a fun or happy event. It can be a memory of a sad event or a time when the parent was naughty as a child. This allows the children to see that their parents are fellow humans and that they have sad or naughty memories too. This game can be a great leveller for children because it enables them to see that their parents can also make mistakes.

Time Masks

In this game you make a mask with your child that represents how she feels at the time. Discuss different feelings with her and then at another time, perhaps four weeks later, do another mask depicting her feelings and compare the two to highlight how we have 'good days' and 'bad days' or whatever comes to light from the different masks you have made.

My Friend

You and your child draw or paint or model in play dough a close friend. When you've done this, discuss what you like about this person and the qualities they have that make them such a good friend. This can be a useful way of highlighting some of the values discussed in Chapter 8. You may value your friend for their honesty and high level of integrity. This can encourage the child to embody those values in her life.

Likes and Dislikes

Using paint, crayons, magazines, postcards, and so on, make a collage of a person that you like and a person that you don't like. Discuss the differences between liking and disliking someone and what they mean. This is an excellent activity for teaching children to determine pros and cons. It also helps them identify the qualities they would like to have in a friend. As with the game above, this is useful for teaching the values mentioned in Chapter 8.

Facing Fears

Ask your child to paint or draw her worst fear or fears and then discuss with her how she might handle them. Other versions of this include giving the child a scenario such as:

- being lost in the desert
- being stuck on a desert island
- being held in a prison
- being kidnapped

This activity is useful for discovering the personal resources that the child might need to handle their fears in a difficult situation. Discussion of fears usually provides the child with strength to draw upon and a sense that even if some of their fears are realised, then they would know how to deal with them. The expression of their fears in this activity also lets them see that they are not the only person who is, for example, scared of the dark or school exams.

Life Story

Take a piece of paper and divide it into 10 sections. Then ask your child to draw a cartoon, frame by frame, of her life story. She can then tell you the story of her life using the strip cartoon. This encourages children to review the good and bad things that have happened in their lives. It can be a useful talking point for sorting out issues that are unresolved.

Survival

Each person draws a suitcase, and then inside the suitcase draws pictures of all of the things they would consider important to take with them if they were shipwrecked on an island. Take turns to discuss the use and value of each item. Why is each object in the suitcase? What will it be used for? This is a great activity for letting children use their imaginative and deductive powers. They really have to think in order to play this game. It provides them with an awareness again of how each person is different and values different things.

Three Wishes

Using clay or play dough, each person makes a model of the three things they would like most if they were given three wishes. Once again, this game encourages children to explore what their highest values are, in other words, what is most important to them in life.

Winning a Lottery

If you won the lottery, what would you spend the money on? Using crayons, ask your child to draw the items she would spend her money on. This game is useful for exploring the issues of trust and unselfishness. Would your child tell other people that she had won the lottery? Would she spend all the money on herself or would she be generous to other people? This discussion can prove to be a very valuable one.

Magic Carpet Ride

If you were given a magic carpet where would you fly to? Ask your child to draw a mural of all of the places she would visit on the magic carpet and then describe them to you. This is an excellent game for developing imagination and verbal communication skills. You may be surprised by just how much knowledge your child has of this world and beyond.

Mind Map

Ask your child to paint or draw a series of people or things that are currently or have been very important in her life. Once again this clarifies the child's values and allows her to realise how important certain people are in her life.

Parent Shopping

Ask your child to write an advertisement to sell her parents as terrific parents to other children. You as the parent write an advertisement to sell your terrific child to other parents. Make sure that the child understands that this is just for fun and that you have no intention of selling her to anyone or letting her sell you. Once you have written your advertisements, discuss them. This is great for letting your child know just how much you value her and all the things that you appreciate about her. It provides her with the opportunity to do the same for you and reminds both of you how important you are to each other.

Sell Yourself

Write an advertisement to sell yourself as the perfect child and the perfect parent. Present this to the rest of the family. This is a fun way of building positive self-image and self-esteem.

Snakes and Ladders of Life

On a large piece of paper, as a group paint a large board game of snakes and ladders. Use some of the events in your life in the game. For example, someone might land on a square that says 'You had a beautiful baby girl called ..., move forward two spaces' or 'You kicked a soccer ball through the lounge room window, go back five places.' This game is great fun as the children get to set the reward squares and the punishment squares, which provides them with an understanding of the concept of rewards and consequences. It also allows them to learn some of the events that have happened in their parents' lives.

The Future Me

Draw, paint or make a collage of how you will look in 10 years' time. Tell your family the characteristics that you will have, what you have done and what your life is like 10 years into the future. This activity is wonderful because it allows the child to make choices about the personal qualities she would like to have when she is older. It also allows her to decide what will be important to her as she grows up. You may need to give your child some assistance with this game, but it is worth the effort.

Key Points

❖ A variety of games can be used to stimulate both verbal and non-verbal communication, imagination, clarification of values, and the boosting of self-image and self-esteem.

❖ Use old junk mail and other items that you would normally recycle, such as toilet rolls, wool, empty boxes, nuts and bolts, as a resource for the games and activities in this chapter.

❖ These activities do not take very long, so you can schedule one or two a week in order to spend special time with your children or each child individually.

❖ The games and activities give you an opportunity to relive your childhood, and in doing so, they allow you to establish better rapport with your own child. This will draw you closer together to create a more intimate relationship.

❖ Such activities provide an opportunity for taking another look at any unresolved issues that exist between family members. Nearly all the games and activities require a 'debriefing' discussion period.

❖ Many of these games and activities can be used to explore the values discussed in Chapter 8.